Simply Spice

Homemade Indian
Vegetarian Food

Simply Spice

Homemade Indian Vegetarian Food

Raji Sharma

First published in 2015 by New Holland Publishers Pty Ltd
London • Sydney • Auckland

The Chandlery Unit 009 50 Westminster Bridge Road London SE1 7QY United Kingdom
1/66 Gibbes Street Chatswood NSW 2067 Australia
5/39 Woodside Ave Northcote, Auckland 0627 New Zealand

www.newhollandpublishers.com

A record of this book is held at the British Library and the National Library of Australia.

ISBN 9781742577494

Managing Director: Fiona Schultz
Publisher: Diane Ward
Project Editor: Holly Willsher
Photography: Suc Stubbs
Stylist: Jodi Wuestewald
Designer: Lorena Susak
Typesetter: Peter Guo
Production Director: Olga Dementiev
Printer: Toppan Leefung Printing Limited

10 9 8 7 6 5 4 3 2 1

Keep up with New Holland Publishers on Facebook
www.facebook.com/NewHollandPublishers

Contents

Dedication

I would love to dedicate this book to: my parents who taught me everything about cooking; my kids Mahesh and Sandhya who are constant source of support and inspiration; and my wonderful friends, particularly the ever optimistic Sylvia, who have become my second family.

Introduction

As a child, my family would travel to Tirunelveli in Southern India every summer to visit my grandmother. She lived in the Brahmin quarter of a small village where lines of mud brick houses led to a small temple in the centre of the town. I remember how Kamala – the family cow – was milked each morning. Her warm, frothy milk was used throughout the day: to make coffee in the morning, soured into yogurt in the afternoon and finally churned into butter, which would later become ghee.

In my family home in Chennai, the kitchen was where I used to spend most of my time. I first learnt the magic of cooking while following my mum around the house – sitting on the floor chopping vegetables until it was finally time to gather around our simple wood fire stove and prepare meals for the day.

My dad took a more intellectual approach to cooking. He would explain the Ayurvedic health benefits behind certain ingredients and spices and what to eat for good health. As an officer in the state police force, my dad also travelled for work and brought back vivid descriptions of foods he tasted on his travels. He would then recite them to my mum so she could recreate the dishes for the whole family.

It was through these everyday experiences that I developed my love for food. From using every last drop of Kamala's milk to perfecting flavors with my parents, my time in India laid the foundations for the food I now cook.

In this book you will discover authentic recipes handed down from my parents and ones that I have picked up along the way. Lots will seem unfamiliar, but take a leap and trust that the flavors will both surprise and delight you.

How To Use This Book

My intention for this cookbook has always been about sharing the true nature of Indian food.

This might be your first experience of Indian cooking, or you might be well acquainted with the world of spices. Whether you start simple or dive into the more complex, this book will be a great companion to deepen your experience of Indian food. Start by following the recipes to understand what spice combinations create what flavors, but as you grow more comfortable with these new ingredients adjust and experiment to create the food that you love.

If you have the time and interest it's always better – and surprisingly easy – to make things from scratch, however there are always store bought alternatives if you prefer to do things quicker.

Some ingredients might also be new to you, or you might just need a refresher, so be sure to read the section on *Setting up an Indian Kitchen* **(page 11)** just to familiarize yourself with the kind of spices and ingredients used in this book.

To give you a sense of how we eat, I've also put together a little guide about how to put meals together on **page 21–23**.

Setting Up Your Indian Kitchen

India is made up of 29 states and 24 (official!) languages, but what distinguishes people even more is how they cook and what they eat.

What you'll mostly find in this book comes from Tamilnadu, the region where I am from. It's a vegetarian cuisine known for delights such as dosai (page 218) and it's use of tamarind, coconut, curry leaves and mustard seeds. The recipes in here also represent my Dad's two sides: a man steeped in the traditions of Ayurveda and Hinduism; and his open mindedness to other tastes and flavors from different regions around the country.

I also wanted to quickly say something about chilli. Indian food can quickly conjure up images of watery eyes and burning mouths. But spices that are balanced and cooked in the right way, create a range of flavors and aromas that are so much more than just being chilli. Recipes in this book sometimes call for chilli, which add a touch of heat to complement other flavors, but if it doesn't suit your palette you can leave it out and still have a great tasting dish.

To get started, it's important to have the right ingredients on hand. Over the page I have listed and described spices and ingredients you'll find in this book that might be new to you. Have a read, take a visit to your local Indian store or good green grocer, stock up on the basics and then you'll be well equipped to cook anything in this book.

See this as a start of an adventure. Explore with open eyes, smell with curiosity and of course eat with pleasure.

Spices

Spices are the heart of Indian cooking. Each spice has it's own unique qualities, and when cooked in the right way really draws out that flavor.

Storing spices in an accessible spot is crucial for Indian cooking. Spice boxes, a round stainless steel container that houses 8 or 9 small tins, are a great way to keep all the basics on hand, failing that 100 gram glass jars also do the trick. If you are getting a spice box make sure you get one with individual lids on tins, as ones without will lose flavor.

I keep small amounts of the spice in the tins or jars and then store anything left in the packet in the pantry in large airtight containers, topping up the jars as needed. Excess freshly ground sambar powder and garam masala should be kept in a zip lock bag in the freezer to maintain freshness.

Basic Spice Set

Asafoetida
This off white powder has a pungent smell that can be overpowering, but when cooked in oil it's fragrant and enhances the flavor of the dish. It comes from a gum of a giant fennel like plant, and in its powdered form is usually cut with rice flour. It has many health properties including aiding digestion and fighting influenza.

Brown or Black Mustard Seeds
When heated in oil and popped these seeds impart a nutty and earthy flavor, often used in combination with curry leaves, urad dhal and asafoetida.

Channa Dhal
A baby chickpea that's been split and polished, commonly used in spice blends, tempered in rice and vegetable dishes and ground to make masala vadas **(page 41)**. Yellow split peas can make a good substitute.

Chilli Powder
Hot chilli powder from red chillies is what to use for Indian cooking.

Cilantro (Coriander) Powder
Cilantro gets used in its seed, herb and powder form. It's delicate flavor is used in many North Indian dishes, you can grind it fresh yourself as needed or buy it in the powdered form.

Cumin Seeds
A delicate and fragrant spice used to flavor rice and dhals.

Garam Masala
Perhaps the most well known Indian spice blend, it's from the North and adds a unique flavor to their curries. There are countless ways to make garam masala, you can easily grind it fresh for yourself using my recipe (page 284) or buy a good quality, freshly ground brand from a whole food or Indian store.

Sambar Powder
A versatile powder used in South Indian curries and vegetable dishes. It's easy to grind yourself, make a big batch then store in a small tin or jar, place the remaining in a zip lock bag and store in the freezer for freshness. You can also buy it from a good Indian store, just check the ingredients and pick one that uses spices close to my recipe (page 285).

Turmeric Powder
Adds a wonderful aroma and color to dhals and vegetables, it's also a powerful antioxidant and immunity booster.

Urad Dhal skinned and split
Urad dhal is tempered and used with vegetables and curries, whole urad dhal is a main ingredient for making dosai (page 218) a fermented lentil pancake that's highly nutritious.

Other Spices to Have Around

Cilantro (Coriander) Seeds
Beautifully aromatic, when freshly pounded and added to curry like Khadi (page 120) they really steal the show.

Dried Red Chillies (hot)
Use a hot variety to add a nice bit of heat to dishes, often simply broken in half and tempered with other spices to gently impart heat.

Dried Methi Leaves or Dried Fenugreek Leaves
These leaves have a pungent fragrance and absolutely transform the flavor of a dish. Rather than cooking in oil with other spices, these are often rubbed between palms and stirred in at the end.

Fenugreek Seeds
These aromatic pungent seeds are added to curries to add depth of flavor.

Lentils
Lentils are the centre piece of any Indian vegetarian diet. High in nutritional value, but also toasted, ground and boiled to make delicious curries, snacks and even desserts.
Red Lentils the most versatile and easiest lentil to cook, you can pick these up at most supermarkets.

Toor Dhal
Also known as pigeon pea, a firmer dhal that takes longer to cook but produces a more dense and creamy dhal, it tastes great in traditional Sambar (page 131).

Channa Dhal
A baby chickpea that's been split, it can be used in many different ways in cooking, tempered to flavor Lemon Rice (page 192), cooked to make a Mixed Lentil Dhal (page 78) or ground and fried to make Masala Vada (page 41).

Mung Beans
Green mung beans are native to India and are used in dhal but also like other lentils they are ground to make pancakes like Pesarattu (page 227).

Yellow Moong Dhal
These are mung beans that have been skinned and split, they're much quicker to cook and used to make koottus.

Flour

Atta Flour
Ground durum wheat uses the two parts of the wheat (endosperm and germ) that are healthy and digestible. If you can't get atta flour you can use equal portions of wholemeal and plain flour that roughly gets you the same constitution.

Besan Flour
Ground channa dhal, a versatile flour that gets used to make Pakoras (page 44) and Bajji's, curries like Khadi (page 120), and the sweet Mysorepak (page 259).

Other Indian Ingredients

Dried Tamarind
A sour fruit, you can buy this in packets from Indian stores. Typically soaked and squeezed then the juice is used in curries. You can also use tamarind paste but only use the paste in much smaller quantities.

Freshly Grated Coconut
A key ingredient in South Indian cooking. You can grate your own **(page 280)** or buy frozen packets from the Indian store. Desiccated coconut is an adequate substitute, if using make sure to soak in warm water to soften.

Green Chilli
Small hot green chillies are used frequently in Indian cooking, often added whole and removed at the end just so they impart a bit of heat.

Paneer
An Indian style of ricotta cheese, very simple to make **(page 277)**, or Indian stores usually sell the best quality products.

Ghee
A kind of clarified butter, the butter is simmered and the milk solids separate leaving golden pure butter fat used in cooking. It's simple and easy to make yourself, see recipe **on page 276**. According to traditional Indian medicine it has many health benefits.

Curry Leaves
An essential ingredient in South Indian cooking, they're extremely aromatic and impart a unique flavor. Well stocked supermarkets sometimes sell these, otherwise the Indian store will definitely have some. You can also plant one in your backyard, it grows into a lovely leafy tree. Fresh is the best way to use this herb, but you can use dried or frozen if that's all you have.

A note on equipment

Frying Pans
In India there are all sorts of traditional pans and tools, I've found the best pans to use are heavy based non-stick pans because they cook the vegetables evenly and also prevent

vegetables and spices sticking and burning to the pan. I have three kinds of pans I most regularly use, a deep frying pan, a flat frying pan with a 10 cm (4 in) rim and a small tempering pan, all of them have lids that can be put on for cooking.

Saucepans

To cook dhal, rice and curries you need good saucepans. I use heavy based stainless steel saucepans with lids, the heaviness is really important as spices will burn quickly while toasting if the base is too thin. I have small, medium and large sizes.

Blender and a Spice Grinder

In India we have a grinder called a "mixie" which is basically a powerful blender with two attachments, one for grinding spices and the other for processing batters for Dosai and Vada. You can buy small spice grinders or even use a coffee grinder for grinding spices, and use a powerful blender for grinding batters.

Coconut Scrapper

If you are keen to scrape your own coconut, the easiest way to do it is buying a coconut scrapper. Most Indian stores will have these, be careful though as the blades are usually extremely sharp. See page 280 for more detail.

Creating Indian meals

For Indians the way we eat a meal is almost as meticulous as the way food is prepared. Whether it's breakfast, lunch or dinner, dishes have been particularly selected, arranged and ordered to create a completely satisfying meal.

Although I don't expect you will be preparing meals in exactly the same way, there are certain rules of thumb that can help you create great meals.

Below I've listed the dishes whose flavors and textures work well together. Cook one or two dishes from each of the categories to make a complete meal. You could also add any snack or chaat dish as a starter, and a sweet like Shrikhand, Carrot Halwa or Gulab Jamun to finish the meal.

An Everyday South Indian Meal

Curry	Vegetables	Serve with
Rasam (page 105)	Avial (page 115)	Steamed rice and a dollop of yogurt on the side.
Poondu Rasam (page 72)	Beans Usili (page 138)	
Easy Sambar (page 92)	Cabbage Thoran (page164)	
Traditional Sambar (page 131)	Spicy Fried Eggplant (page 157)	For the full south Indian experience start with Rasam, then to another curry and finish with Yogurt Rice (page 195).
Keerai Koottu (page 75)	Potato and Snake Beans (page 158)	
Pumpkin and Black-Eyed Peas Koottu (page 82)	Spicy Potato Fry (page 166)	
Morkuzhambu (page 123)	Stuffed Eggplant (page 144)	
Theeyal (page 126)		
Pulikuzhambu (page 128)		

A Simple North Indian Meal

Curry	Vegetables	Serve with
Simple Dhal (page 98)	Bindi Masala (page 142)	Steamed rice, a simple pulao or indian bread.
Rajma (page 96)	Eggplant and Zucchini Masala (page 160)	
Sodhi (page 86)		Jeera Pulao (page 206)
Mixed Lentil Dhal (page 78)	Aloo Masala (page 162)	Peas and Mint Pulao (page 207)
Matar Paneer (page 103)	Baingan Bharta (page 152)	Indian Fried Rice (page 204)
		Chapati (page 178)
		Paratha (page 170)

Special Meals to Share with Family and Friends

Curry	Vegetables	Serve with
Khadi (page 120)	Spicy Potato Fry (page 166)	A simple Pulao and Raita
Paneer Kofta Curry (page 110)	Dry Fried Okra (page 142)	Jeera Pulao (page 206)
Palak Paneer (page 134)	Stuffed Eggplant (page 144)	Peas and Mint Pulao (page 207)
Vegetable Kurma (page 108)		Indian Fried Rice (page 204)
		Mixed Raita (page 241)
		Mint Raita (page 241)

Indian Brunch or Light Supper

These combinations are eaten mostly in the south as "tiffin" which is usually brunch or early afternoon, they make a beautiful light meal.

- Dosai (page 218) with easy or traditional Sambar (page 131) and Coconut Chutney (page 242)
- Adai (page 224) with Morkuzhambu (page 123) or just a bit of honey
- Pesarattu (page 227) with Tomato Chutney (page 244)
- Thakali Dosai (page 222) with easy or traditional Sambar (page 131)

- Puri (page 181) and Masala Potato (page 147)
- Masala Dosai (page 220) served with a side of Sambar (page 131) and Coconut Chutney (page 242)
- Chapati (page 178) or Paratha (page 170) with Aloo Masala (page 162), Vegetable Kurma (page 108) or quick Cauliflower Kurma (page 88), with Raita (page 240) on the side

A Special Dinner Party

Snacks	Curry	Serve with	Sweet
Paneer Samosa (page 46) Sev Puri (page 62) Grilled Paneer Skewers (page 51)	Khadi (page 120) Paneer Kofta Curry (page 110) Palak Paneer (page 134) Vegetable Kurma (page 108)	A simple Pulao and Raita Jeera Pulao (page 206) Peas and Mint Pulao (page 207) Indian Fried Rice (page 204) Mixed or Mint Raita (page 241)	Gulab Jamun (page 254) Carrot Halwa (page 252) Shrikhand (page 262)

For guests when they pop in
- Pakoras (page 44)
- Bajji (page 39)
- Mysorepak (page 259) and Milky Sweet Chai (page 268)

Biryani Feast

Curry	Vegetables	Serve with
Vegetable Biryani (page 211)	Vegetable Kurma (page 108) Quick Cauliflower Kurma (page 88) Matar Paneer (page 103)	Mixed Raita (page 241) Mint Raita (page 241) Carrot Salad (page 234) Papaya Salad (page 232)

Snacks

South Indian Potato and Pea Samosa

Makes: 15 Samosas
Cooking Difficulty: Easy

A simple samosa served in the south using spring roll wrappers instead of pastry. Serve with mint, cilantro and coconut chutney (page 56), tomato or chilli sauce.

Ingredients
1 tablespoon canola oil
1 medium onion, finely chopped
2 cloves garlic, finely diced
2.5 cm (1 in) piece ginger, finely diced
1 teaspoon garam masala
¼ teaspoon turmeric powder
¼ teaspoon chilli powder
2 tablespoons water
1 teaspoon salt
2 large potatoes, boiled, peeled and cut into 1 cm (½ in) cubes
60 g (2 oz) peas, fresh or frozen
¼ teaspoon cilantro (coriander) seeds, coarsely ground
Frozen spring roll pastry, thawed
2 tablespoons water mixed with 1 teaspoon plain flour (for assembling samosas)
Canola oil for deep frying

Method
Heat the oil in a deep frying pan on a medium-high heat. Add the onion, garlic and ginger cook for 2 minutes until the onion lightly browns. Add all the spices, (except the ground cilantro), water and salt and stir for a few minutes to make a paste. Now add the potatoes and peas, stir together until the potatoes are well coated with the spice mix. Sprinkle with the coarse cilantro powder, stir. Mash the mixture together so the potatoes and peas are

squashed but still a bit chunky. Lower the heat and cook for 5 minutes, stir occasionally. Transfer to a bowl to cool.

To assemble the samosas cut a pastry sheet into three long strips (if you have individual size spring roll squares cut in half, into two long strips). Place 1 tablespoon of potato mix on one end of a pastry strip. Gently fold one corner up to make a triangle shape, then keep folding the triangle, sealing the edges with a bit of the flour/water liquid. By the end of the strip you should have a perfectly wrapped triangle. Place on a plate covered with damp cloth, then make the rest of the samosas.

To cook the samosas, fill a deep frying pan two thirds full with canola oil. Heat oil on medium-high heat, when ready the surface will shimmer it shouldn't smoke. To test if the oil is hot, drop a small bit of pastry into the oil, if it slowly sizzles that's the right temperature. Add 3 to 4 samosas at a time, gently turning frequently, cook until golden brown. Using a slotted spoon lift the samosas out, drain any excess oil and place on a plate lined with paper towel.

Chundal
(Chickpea and Ginger Salad)

Serves: 4 to 6 as a snack
Cooking Difficulty: Easy

When visiting the temple, chundal is often a dish that is prepared blessed by the gods, then shared with the devoted masses. It's also just a nourishing healthy snack, light and moreish because of the ginger and coconut.

Ingredients
2 teaspoons canola oil
½ teaspoon black mustard seeds
2 whole dried red chillies, roughly torn
5 cm (2 in) piece ginger, finely diced
15 fresh curry leaves
330 g (11.6 oz) cooked chickpeas*
1 carrot, coarsely grated
1 tablespoon desiccated or fresh grated coconut **(page 280)**
¼ teaspoon salt
10 g (0.5 oz) cilantro (coriander), stalks and leaves finely chopped

*If you are using dried chickpeas soak 70 g (2.4 oz) dried chickpeas in cold water overnight. Cook with plenty of water in a saucepan until soft. Or use 2 cans of chickpeas with no added sugar.

Method
Heat the oil in a large non-stick frying pan on a medium heat. Add the mustard seeds, when they start to pop, add the dried chillies, ginger and curry leaves, stir for a minute.

Add cooked chickpeas, carrot, coconut and salt and stir for another minute. Lower the heat, cover the pan, cook for few minutes.

Remove from the heat, sprinkle with cilantro leaves and transfer to a serving bowl.

Bonda
(Spicy Battered Potato Balls)

Makes: 10–15 Bondas
Cooking Difficulty: Medium

Spicy potato mash rolled into a ball, dipped into a batter made from besan flour and gently fried until golden brown. There are a few steps in the process, but they're all straightforward and it's definitely worth it for the end product.

These bondas are also used as the filling for a Vada Pav (page 68), so if you really want to wow guests you could try your hand at that. Otherwise these are perfectly delicious served with Coconut Chutney (page 242) or even tomato sauce.

Ingredients
For the filling
½ teaspoon black mustard seeds
1 tablespoon roughly chopped cashew nuts
1½ teaspoons urad dhal
1½ teaspoons channa dhal or yellow split peas
15 curry leaves, roughly torn
1 small hot green chilli, finely chopped
2.5 cm (1 in) piece ginger, finely grated
¼ teaspoon turmeric powder
2 medium potatoes, boiled and cubed
1 teaspoon salt
60 ml (2 fl oz) water
1 teaspoon lemon juice
2 tablespoons cilantro (coriander), stalks and leaves finely chopped

continued over the page...

For the batter
130 g (4.6 oz) besan flour (chickpea flour found at Indian stores)
120 ml (4 fl oz) soda water
¼ teaspoon chilli powder
Pinch of asafoetida
½ teaspoon salt

Canola oil for deep frying

Method

For the filling
Heat oil in a deep frying pan on a medium-high heat. Add the mustard seeds, when they pop immediately add the cashew nuts, urad dhal and channa dhal stir until slightly brown. Then add the curry leaves, chillies, ginger and turmeric powder stirring for 10 seconds. Add the boiled potatoes and salt, stir well. Pour in 60 ml (2 fl oz) of water, stir well. Roughly mash the potatoes with a fork so it's half mashed and half chunky. Finally stir through the lemon juice and cilantro leaves. Transfer to a bowl to cool.

Once cool, roll 2 tablespoons of the potato mix into a ball, place on a plate. Repeat with the remaining mix.

For the batter
In a large bowl mix all the ingredients for the batter and whisk until smooth.

Frying the bondas
Fill a deep frying pan two thirds full with canola oil, heat on a medium-high heat. Check if the oil is hot by dropping a small amount of batter in the oil, if it immediately sizzles it's the correct temperature. Lower the heat slightly to maintain this temperature.

Gently place potato balls, one at a time, in the batter until completely coated. Gently drop bonda into the oil, cooking 4 to 5 at a time. Use a slotted spoon to gently turn the bondas, until golden brown. Drain and place on a plate lined with paper towel. Repeat for remaining bondas.

Allow the bondas to cool a little before serving.

Raji's Vegetable Cutlet

Makes: 15–18

Cooking Difficulty: Medium

This is a snack that Indians love, but I never seemed to eat one that I liked, they were either too oily or too spicy, never quite right. So I went back to my kitchen and tried my hand at making them just right.

I guess the proof is in the pudding, as every time I go back to my family's home in India my nieces and nephews always beg me to make it, so if the Indians love it, it must be good. Perfect with tomato ketchup or Mint Raita (page 241).

Ingredients

2 tablespoons canola oil
1 large onion, finely diced
2 cloves garlic, finely grated
5 cm (2 in) piece of ginger, finely grated
½ teaspoon garam masala
½ teaspoon cumin powder
¼ teaspoon chilli powder
¼ teaspoon turmeric powder
2 large potatoes, cut in 1 cm (½ in) dice
1 medium carrot, cut in 1 cm (½ in) dice
60 g (2 oz) green peas
½ teaspoon salt
4 tablespoons cilantro (coriander), stalks and leaves finely chopped
300 g (10.5 oz) breadcrumbs
120 ml (4 fl oz) water
4 tablespoons plain flour
Canola oil for deep frying

continued over the page...

Method

Heat oil in a large frying pan on a medium heat. Add the onion, garlic and ginger and stir until the onion is soft and slightly changes color. Then add all the dry spices and stir for a few seconds. Now add all the vegetables and salt, stir well. Turn the heat down a little, cover the pan with a lid and cook the vegetables for 10 minutes until soft, stirring occasionally. Once cooked, taste for salt and adjust as needed. Add chopped cilantro and turn off the heat.

Using a potato masher gently mash everything together so it's half soft and half chunky. Transfer to a bowl, cover and chill in the fridge for 1 hour.

Once the vegetable mix has cooled, take two tablespoons and using your hands shape them into small 6 cm (2½ in) oval size patties. You should get about 15 to 18 patties.

In a small bowl, mix plain flour with water to make a thick liquid almost like thick milk, and pour the breadcrumbs on a plate. Dip each patty into the thick liquid and then immediately place on the breadcrumb plate so it's completely coated. Place the covered patties on a dry plate. Continue this process for the rest of the patties. Then repeat the process again so all the patties have been covered twice, this will give you a nice crunchy patty. If you run out of flour liquid make extra and add more breadcrumbs as needed.

Fill a deep frying pan two thirds full with canola oil, heat on a medium-high heat. The oil should be hot but not smoking, and the cutlets should sizzle when they're in the pan. Cook 4 to 5 patties in the oil at a time, turning occasionally until they're golden brown all over. Use a slotted spoon to remove and drain on paper towel.

Eat with your favorite chutney or sauce.

Note: crumbed patties store well in the freezer, so you can cook as needed.

Paneer Stuffed Chilli Bajji

Makes: 6 Bajjis
Cooking Difficulty: Easy

Banana chillies are ideal for this, but if they're not in season you could also try baby bell peppers (capsicum). Serve with your favorite chutney or tomato sauce.

Ingredients
For the batter
130 g (4.6 oz) besan flour
120 ml (4 fl oz) water
½ teaspoon salt
¼ teaspoon baking powder
¼ teaspoon chilli powder

For paneer stuffing
100 g (3.5 oz) paneer or ricotta, crumbled
¼ teaspoon cumin powder
¼ teaspoon turmeric powder
½ teaspoon salt
1 tablespoon cilantro (coriander), leaves and stalks finely chopped

6 long banana chillies or baby bell peppers (capsicums)

Canola oil for deep frying

continued over the page...

Method

Mix all the dry ingredients for the batter in a mixing bowl, then whisk in the water to make a smooth batter. Set aside.

Mix all the ingredients for the stuffing in a bowl. If you're using ricotta for the stuffing take care to drain well so it's not too watery. Set aside.

Make a long cut through the chilli or pepper and remove all the seeds. Gently pull the sides apart and stuff with 1 tablespoon or so of paneer stuffing, bring the sides back together tightly. Repeat with remaining chillies.

Fill a deep frying pan two thirds full with canola oil, heat on a medium-high heat. To test if the oil is hot, drop a tiny bit of batter into the oil, if the batter bubbles and rises to the top it's just right, if the batter burns or there's smoke it's too hot and you'll need to reduce the heat to bring the temperature down. Maintain this temperature.

Take one stuffed chilli and completely submerge in the batter, then gently ease the chilli into the hot oil, cook 3 at a time. Once cooked a little, gently turn to ensure they cook evenly, until golden brown. Scoop out and drain on paper towel.

Allow to cool before you dig in.

Vegetable Bajjis

Serves: 4–6
Cooking Difficulty: Easy

Bajji's are a quick and tasty snack usually whipped up for hungry kids after school or unexpected guests, because there's no way you can enter an Indian home and not get fed. Once you know how to make the batter, use whatever vegetables you have around. Serve with Coconut Chutney (page 242).

Ingredients
For the batter
130 g (4.6 oz) besan flour (chickpea flour, available at Indian store)
½ teaspoon baking powder
½ teaspoon salt
¼ teaspoon chilli powder
120 ml (4 fl oz) water

For the vegetables
1 large potato
1 large red onion
1 large eggplant (aubergine)

Canola oil for deep frying

continued over the page...

Method

First prepare the batter. In a large bowl, mix all the dry ingredients together, then whisk in the water to make a smooth batter. Set aside.

Peel the potato and onion, then cut the potato, onion and eggplant into ½ cm (0.2 in) round slices. Pat the vegetables with a paper towel to remove excess water, which will ensure they stay crispy when cooked.

Fill a deep frying pan two thirds full with canola oil, heat on a medium-high heat. To test if the oil is hot, drop a tiny bit of batter into the oil, if the batter bubbles and rises to the top it's just right, if the batter burns or there's smoke it's too hot and you'll need to reduce the heat to bring the temperature down. Maintain this temperature.

Using your hand take a vegetable slice, completely dip it into the thick batter and then gently ease the slice into the hot oil, don't overcrowd the pan. Once the batter is golden brown gently turn the bhaji over to cook the other side. Scoop out and drain on paper towel. Repeat for the rest of the vegetables.

Masala Vada

(Lentil Fritters)

Makes: 12–16
Cooking Difficulty: Easy

A traditional South Indian snack eaten on special occasions, specially prepared as an offering to the gods, or just bought at the humble street stall selling "tea and vada" to the masses.

Ingredients
200 g (7 oz) channa dhal or yellow split peas
2–4 dried red chillies (adjust to taste)
2–4 tablespoon water
½ teaspoon salt
1 large red onion, finely chopped
10 curry leaves, roughly torn
5 tablespoons cilantro (coriander), leaves and stalks finely chopped
Oil for deep frying

Method
Soak channa dhal with dried chillies for 2 to 3 hours. Wash and drain thoroughly.

Place channa dhal, chillies with salt and water in a food processor and process to a coarse mixture. Transfer to a large bowl. Add onion, curry leaves and cilantro, mix well.

Take a small handful of lentil mix (about 1½ tablespoons) and using your hands make a round patty. Make all the patties and place them on a plate.

Fill a deep frying pan two thirds full with canola oil, heat on a medium-high heat. Drop a small amount of ground lentil mix to test the oil temperature. If it starts to sizzle immediately, this is the correct temperature. Lower the heat slightly to maintain this temperature.

continued over the page...

Gently cook 4 to 5 patties at a time until the patties are a deep golden brown on both sides. Use a slotted spoon to remove vadas and drain on paper towel. While cooking, if the oil starts to smoke it's too hot. Remove pan from the heat and allow the oil to cool slightly before bringing it back on a lowered heat.

Allow to cool slightly before eating so the centre of the vada sets.

You can freeze the ground lentil mix and defrost to make these vadas as needed.

Pakoras

(Chickpea Flour Fritters with Onion and Cilantro)

Serves: 4 as a starter
Cooking Difficulty: Easy

Pakoras are a snack that need no introduction, these little fritters have made their way onto menus at most Indian restaurants. Once you realize how easy they are to prepare, you'll be making them all the time. This recipe is for a simple onion and carrot pakora, but you can throw in any grated vegetable – potato, carrot and zucchini (courgette) would all work well.

Ingredients

130 g (4.6 oz) besan flour (chickpea flour available at Indian stores)
1 tablespoon rice flour
½ teaspoon chilli powder
½ teaspoon salt
1 large red onion, finely sliced
6 tablespoons cilantro (coriander), stalks and leaves finely sliced
120 ml (4 fl oz) water
Canola oil for deep frying

Method

Mix all the ingredients, except the water and oil, in a large bowl. Slowly add the water and mix to form a batter, you want everything to be well coated in the flour and for it to be wet and sticky. If the batter is too runny add more besan flour, if it's too dry add more water.

Fill a deep frying pan two thirds full with canola oil, heat on a medium-high heat. To test if the oil is the right temperature, drop a tiny bit of batter into the oil, if the batter bubbles and rises to the top it's just right, if the batter sinks to the bottom wait until the oil gets hotter; if it burns and smokes it's too hot, reduce the heat.

Use your hands, or a spoon, to scoop about a tablespoon of the mix. Gently drop into the oil. Fry about 10 to 15 pakoras at one time, turning them over so they brown all over. When golden brown, drain from the oil with a slotted spoon and place on paper towel. Repeat the same process with the rest of the batter.

Paneer Samosa

Makes: 10–15 Samosas
Cooking Difficulty: Easy

I've started a tradition of hosting a Christmas Eve party, inviting friends over for small snacks and drinks. I wanted to try something new so decided to make my own paneer samosas. Everyone loved it so I think I'll have to make them every year. If you have the time this would be a really nice way to use fresh paneer (page 277).

Serve with Mint Raita (page 241) and sliced cucumber.

Ingredients
1 tablespoon canola oil
1 medium onion, finely chopped
2.5 cm (1 in) piece ginger, finely diced
1 small hot green chilli, finely chopped
1 teaspoon garam masala **(page 284)**
¼ teaspoon turmeric powder
1 tomato, seeds removed and finely chopped
½ teaspoon salt
200 g (7 oz) paneer, grated
¼ teaspoon dried methi leaves (dried fenugreek leaves, available in Indian stores)
2–3 sheets frozen shortcrust pastry, thawed

continued over the page...

Method

Heat the oil in a deep frying pan on medium-high heat. Fry the onion, ginger and chilli for 2 minutes until the onion starts to brown. Add all the spices (except methi leaves), chopped tomatoes and salt, continue to stir for a minute. Now add the grated paneer and stir together until the tomato spice mix are well blended through with paneer. Take methi leaves and rub them between your palms over the spiced paneer filling (rubbing releases the gentle flavor of the methi leaves). Lower heat and cook for 5 minutes, stirring occasionally. Remove from the heat and transfer to a mixing bowl to cool.

Place one pastry sheet on a clean dry cutting board. Cut into 9 equal squares. Have a little bowl of water on the side to help seal the samosa.

To make the samosa take a pastry square in your hand, with your finger dab water on the edges. Bring two opposite corners together and make a cone by sealing an edge together. Fill the cone with 2 tablespoons of the paneer mix, gently push in. To close the samosa fold the open edge over, and starting from one corner pinch and turn to seal and form frills. Place on a plate and cover with a moist tea towel, while you make the rest.

Heat the oil in a deep frying pan over a medium-high heat. To test if the oil is hot, drop a tiny bit of pastry into oil, it should slowly sizzle. Maintain this temperature. Cook 3 to 4 samosas at a time, gently turning so they evenly cook. When golden brown, use a slotted spoon to lift samosas out of the oil, drain and place on a plate lined with paper towel. Cook remaining samosas.

Pao Bhaji
(Spicy Vegetable Mash with Bread)

Serves: 4–6
Cooking Difficulty: Easy

Ask anyone who has lived in Mumbai and they'll rave about the deliciousness of Pao Bhaji. A spicy vegetable mash eaten with sweet breads, that are covered in butter and lightly toasted. It is a rich dish, but eaten occasionally it's a real delight. Eat with soft bread rolls, cucumber and onion.

Ingredients:
For the bhaji (spicy mashed vegetables)
30 g (1 oz) butter
¼ teaspoon cumin seeds
1 red onion, roughly chopped
2 cloves garlic, finely diced
2.5 cm (1 in) piece ginger, finely diced
1 small hot green chilli, deseeded and finely chopped
45 g (1.5 oz) bell pepper (capsicum), finely chopped
2 teaspoons garam masala **(page 284)**
1 teaspoon chilli powder (adjust to taste)
¼ teaspoon turmeric powder
1 large tomato, finely chopped
1 teaspoon salt
2 potatoes, boiled cut in cubes
130 g (4.5 oz) cauliflower florets, boiled cut into small pieces
60 g (2 oz) green peas fresh or frozen, boiled
240 ml (8 fl oz) water
4 tablespoons cilantro (coriander) leaves and stalks finely chopped

Pav (bread)
8 small soft dinner rolls or brioche buns
3 tablespoons butter

Method

Heat the butter in a large non-stick frying pan over a medium heat. Add the cumin seeds and stir for a few seconds so they toast and release their aroma. Then add the onions, garlic and ginger and cook until the onion is soft and slightly translucent. Add the chopped chillies and bell pepper, cook for a minute until the bell pepper is soft.

Add all the spices and stir for a few seconds. Now add the tomatoes and salt, stir for 2 minutes until soft. Add all the boiled vegetables, mash them up and incorporate well with the onion and tomato paste. Add 240 ml (8 fl oz) of water and cook for 2 minutes. Add the cilantro leaves, reserving a little to garnish, lower the heat and simmer for 5 minutes.

Remove from the heat and transfer to a serving dish, garnish with cilantro leaves.

To prepare the bread, slice each roll in half. Heat a large frying pan on medium-high heat for a few minutes. Add 1 tablespoon of butter, when it's melted add a sliced bread roll, cut side down, and cook on one side until it is brown and crispy. You can cook 4 halves in one batch and cook the rest the same way.

Serve immediately, one pav with a small bowl of bhajji, for dipping and eating.

Grilled Paneer Skewers

Makes: 10–15 skewers
Cooking Difficulty: Easy

This is a really nice way to eat paneer and is perfect if you're a vegetarian bringing something to a barbeque, watch all the meat eaters flock to this skewer! If you want to eat it in a more traditional Indian setting the skewers work nicely as a side for Biryani (page 211) or your favorite Pulao.

Ingredients
3 tablespoons thick greek yogurt
2.5 cm (1 in) piece ginger
1 clove of garlic
1 green chilli (adjust to taste)
½ teaspoon cumin powder
¼ teaspoon turmeric powder
½ teaspoon salt
2 teaspoons dried methi leaves (dried fenugreek leaves available at Indian stores)
400 g (14 oz) paneer (**home made page 277** or store bought)
1 green bell pepper (capsicum), cut into chunks
2 red onions, cut into chunks
4–6 tablespoons ghee or canola oil, to cook

15 bamboo skewers, soaked for 30 minutes

continued over the page...

Method

Place yogurt, ginger, garlic, chilli, cumin, turmeric and salt in a spice grinder and process to a fine paste. Add methi leaves and mix.

Cut the paneer into 2.5 cm (1 in) cubes. Completely cover the paneer cubes in the yogurt marinade. Marinate for at least two hours in the fridge.

To make the skewers, alternate with paneer, bell pepper and onion.

To cook the skewers melt the ghee in a small bowl and coat paneer skewers before placing on a hot grill or barbeque. Cook the skewer until nicely charred on all sides, baste with marinade as it's cooking.

Street Food

Chaat

Chaat is the style of street food originating from the streets of Mumbai, but now widely prepared and enjoyed by people all over India. Although the best stuff comes from those street stalls on busy Mumbai streets, it is possible to recreate the flavors and textures yourself.

Chaat dishes often include three chutneys of different colors that balance the flavors of salty, spicy, sweet, sour and astringent. Depending on the type of chaat dish you make there are also different kinds of crunchy textures, from puffed rice or crispy puris.

These two recipes are the two key chaat chutneys: a green mint, cilantro and coconut chutney; and a brown dates and tamarind chutney. The recipes make quite a bit of chutney so you can freeze the excess which makes it super simple to throw your favorite chaat dish together.

Mint, Cilantro and Coconut Chutney

Makes: 150 ml
Cooking Difficulty: Easy

Ingredients
1 bunch cilantro (coriander), stalks and leaves roughly chopped
½ bunch mint leaves, roughly chopped
40 g (1.5 oz) desiccated or fresh grated coconut **(page 280)**
8 whole cashews
3 fresh green chillies
5 cm (2 in) piece ginger
Juice of a lemon
½ teaspoon salt
120 ml (4 fl oz) water

Method
Place all ingredients with 60 ml (2 fl oz) of water in a spice grinder or blender, and process to a coarse paste. Transfer to a bowl and stir through the rest of the water. Check for salt and adjust according to taste.

Sweet Date Chutney

Makes: 200 ml
Cooking Difficulty: Easy

Ingredients
175 g (6.2 oz) pitted dates
1 tablespoon tightly packed dried tamarind
90 g (3.2 oz) jaggery or brown sugar
¼ teaspoon cilantro (coriander) powder
¼ teaspoon cumin powder
¼ teaspoon chilli powder (adjust to taste)

Method
Soak dates in 180 ml (6 fl oz) of warm water for an hour.

Soak the dried tamarind in 120 ml (4 fl oz) of warm to hot water for 10 minutes. Squeeze the softened tamarind with your hand and mix it well in the water, strain through a sieve and set aside.

Place soaked dates with their water, strained tamarind juice, jaggery and spices in a spice grinder or blender, blend to a smooth paste. You should have a consistency of tomato or barbeque sauce.

Store in a clean jar in the fridge for 5 days or the freezer.

Bhel Puri

Makes: 6–8 small bowls as a snack or starter
Cooking Difficulty: Easy

A lively mix of light and crunchy puffed rice with potatoes, onion, cilantro and sweet, sour and chilli chutneys.

Ingredients
400 g (14 oz) puffed rice (available at Indian stores or the health food section)
150 g (5 oz) sev (crispy besan noodles, available at Indian stores)
15 plain rice crackers, roughly broken
1 large red onion, finely diced
4 tablespoons cilantro (coriander), leaves and stems finely chopped
2 potatoes, boiled, peeled and cut into 1 cm (½ in) cubes
6–8 tablespoons sweet date chutney **(page 57)**
4 tablespoons mint, cilantro and coconut chutney **(page 56)**

Method
In a large bowl mix the puffed rice, 100 g (3.5 oz) of the sev and the rice crackers together. Then add onion, half the cilantro leaves and potatoes, mix well. Finally add the date and cilantro chutneys and stir.

Serve immediately in individual small bowls, and sprinkle the remaining sev and cilantro on top to garnish.

Bombay Sandwich

Serves: 4–6
Cooking Difficulty: Easy

The fact there is such a thing as a bombay sandwich is probably an ode to the British Empire. This one is an Indian take on the classic cucumber sandwich. You can also add tomato and onion if you like.

Ingredients
2 medium potatoes
1 teaspoon ghee or canola oil
½ teaspoon cumin powder
½ teaspoon salt
12 slices soft white bread
2 cucumbers, thinly sliced into circles
2 tablespoons mint, cilantro and coconut chutney **(page 56)**

Method
Peel the potatoes and then boil them until just tender. Drain and allow to cool. Once cooled, cut into round circles about ½ cm (0.2 in) thick.

Heat ghee or oil in a frying pan on medium-high heat. Add the potatoes, cumin powder and salt, stir well so the potatoes are evenly coated in the spice. Cook for a few minutes. Remove from heat and allow the potatoes to cool completely.

To prepare the sandwiches, spread one teaspoon of mint, cilantro and coconut chutney on a slice of bread. On another slice, place a layer of cucumbers and then a layer of potatoes. Gently press the two slices of the bread together and cut the sandwich into 4 triangles. Make the rest of the sandwiches in the same way.

Sev Puri

Serves: 6–8
Cooking Difficulty: Easy

If you can manage to get some sev puris (small puffs made from semolina) from the Indian store you'll be able to sample this dish as it's meant to be eaten. You crack the little puffs fill it with potatoes, chutney and eat it all in one mouthful.

This dish is definitely an example of the sum being greater than its parts, eating everything on it's own just doesn't have the same effect as the burst of flavor you get from eating it all together. If you can't get the sev puri puffs we've found carefully piling everything on a plain rice cracker works just as well.

Ingredients
1 teaspoon cooking oil
2 medium potatoes, boiled, peeled and cut into 1 cm (½ in) cubes
¼ teaspoon salt
¼ teaspoon turmeric powder
½ teaspoon cumin powder
120 g (4.5 oz) plain yogurt
1 packet sev puri puffs (bought from the Indian grocer) or 1 packet plain rice crackers
1 medium red onion, finely diced
1 small firm tomato, seeds removed and finely diced
4 tablespoons mint, cilantro and coconut chutney **(page 56)**
4 tablespoons sweet date chutney **(page 57)**
150 g (5 oz) sev (crispy besan noodles, available at Indian stores)
4 tablespoons cilantro (coriander), stalks and leaves finely chopped

continued over the page...

Method

Heat the oil in a non-stick frying pan over a medium heat. Add the boiled potatoes, half the amount of salt, turmeric powder, ¼ teaspoon cumin powder and stir for few minutes until the potatoes start to turn brown. Remove from the heat and cool.

Mix the yogurt, the remaining ¼ teaspoon cumin powder and the remaining salt together, whisk until you get a smooth creamy consistency.

To assemble, if you're using sev puri's arrange on a plate and gently crack the top open using the stem of a spoon. Or if you're using rice crackers simply arrange them on a plate.

You can have a bit of an assembly line with all the ingredients in little bowls. Spoon 1 teaspoon of the potato mix on a cracker or in the puri then sprinkle over the onions and tomato. Pour ½ teaspoon each of each chutney and yogurt sauce. Finish by sprinkling with sev and fresh cilantro.

Eat immediately, popping the whole thing in your mouth at once.

Aloo Tikki

(Spicy Potato Patty with Chutneys)

Makes: 10–12
Cooking Difficulty: Easy

A popular snack all over India, these little potato pattyies are fried until crispy and served with a dollop of all the different Chaat chutney's. Add more green chillies to taste, to really pack a punch.

Ingredients
60 ml (2 fl oz) cooking oil
2 large boiled potatoes, mashed
120 g (4.2 oz) green peas, cooked and mashed
½ teaspoon cumin powder
½ teaspoon cilantro (coriander) powder
4 tablespoons cilantro (coriander), finely chopped
1 green chilli (adjust to taste)
½ teaspoon salt
¼ teaspoon turmeric powder
40 g (1.4 oz) breadcrumbs

For serving:
60 ml (2 fl oz) sweet date chutney **(page 57)**
60 ml (2 fl oz) mint, cilantro and coconut chutney **(page 56)**
60 ml (2 fl oz) natural yogurt, whipped
3 tablespoons cilantro (coriander), finely chopped

continued over the page...

Method

Heat 1 tablespoon of oil in a frying pan on a medium-high heat, add all the ingredients, stir well and cook for a few minutes until everything is well combined.

Transfer to a mixing bowl and refrigerate to cool. When the mixture is cool enough to handle take a large spoonful and shape them into thick, flat round patties, you should get about 10 to 12.

To cook the patties heat 1 tablespoon of oil in a frying pan over medium-high heat. Gently arrange 3 to 4 patties, using a spatula press the patties down a little and cook for 2 minutes. Flip and cook until both sides are golden and crispy. Remove from pan and transfer to a plate lined with paper towel. Cook remaining patties.

To serve, arrange the cooked aloo tikki patties on a platter. Dollop one teaspoon of cilantro chutney on each patty, then drizzle with sweet date chutney, then yogurt and finally top off with cilantro leaves.

Serve each person a pattie to eat, keeping the extra chutney on hand in case people want more.

Vada Pav

(Indian Style Potato Hamburger)

Makes: 6
Cooking Difficulty: Easy

India's answer to the hamburger, a spicy bonda smashed and stuffed into a bun with hot garlic chutney. It takes a few steps to prepare all the different parts but it would definitely impress at a barbeque or if you're having guests for lunch.

Ingredients
6 soft dinner rolls
2 tablespoons red garlic chilli chutney (page 249)
2 tablespoons mint, cilantro and coconut chutney (page 56)
1 cucumber, sliced
1 firm tomato, sliced
1 red onion, finely sliced
6 potato bondas (page 30) or vegetable cutlets (page 33)
2 tablespoons sweet date chutney (page 57)

Method
Slice a bread roll in half and spread a teaspoon of garlic chutney on one half and a teaspoon of cilantro chutney on the other. Arrange a few cucumber, tomato and onion slices on the bottom half of the roll, place a potato bonda or cutlet down next and gently squash it a little. Drizzle over a teaspoon of date chutney and close with the top of the roll.

Gently press down and eat immediately.

Simple Curries

Poondu Rasam

(Spicy Garlic, Tomato and Tamarind Soup)

Serves: 6–8
Cooking Difficulty: Easy

This garlic variety of Rasam (page 105) is especially made, but not restricted to, when people have the cold or the flu. The garlic holds many medicinal properties and when cooked in this way, the pepper and cumin seeds are sure to clear the sinuses, and get you on the path to recovery.

Drink on it's own like a soup, or pour over steamed rice with a dollop of ghee for a nourishing meal. Make a full meal of it and cook Cabbage Thoran (page 164) or some Beans Usili (page 138) on the side.

Ingredients

2 tablespoons dried tamarind or 1 teaspoon tamarind paste
240 ml (8 fl oz) warm water
1½ teaspoons black peppercorns
2 teaspoons cumin seeds
2 dried red chillies (adjust to taste)
1 tablespoon ghee
½ teaspoon black mustard seeds
15 curry leaves, roughly torn
¼ teaspoon asafoetida
700 ml (1½ pints) water
3 ripe tomatoes, chopped in quarters
6 whole cloves garlic, crushed and roughly chopped
1 teaspoon salt
¼ teaspoon turmeric powder
4 tablespoons cilantro (coriander), stalks and leaves finely chopped

continued over the page...

Method

Soak the dried tamarind in 240 ml (8 fl oz) of warm to hot water for 10 minutes. Squeeze the softened tamarind with your hand and mix the fibres well in the water, strain through a fine sieve pushing as much pulp as you can through, set aside. If you're using tamarind paste simply stir it with 240 ml (8 fl oz) of warm water and set aside.

Place the pepper, cumin seeds and red chilli in a spice grinder, and grind into a coarse powder. If you don't have a spice grinder you can pound the ingredients in a mortar and pestle.

Heat the ghee in a large heavy based saucepan on a medium heat. Add the mustard seeds, when they start to pop add the curry leaves, asafoetida and your freshly ground spice powder. Stir to combine, then add 700 ml (1½ pints) water, strained tamarind juice, tomatoes, garlic, salt and turmeric powder.

Bring to the boil, lower the heat slightly and cook for 10 minutes until the tomatoes are completely cooked and soft. Using the back of a spoon crush half the tomatoes a little to release their juices. Turn the heat down and simmer for another 5 minutes.

Remove from heat and stir through cilantro leaves.

Keerai Koottu

(Spinach and Lentil Stew)

Serves: 4–6 as part of a full meal
Cooking Difficulty: Easy

Koottu is a native Tamil dish, that combines a coconut spice blend, different kinds of vegetable and lentils. This recipe uses spinach as the main ingredient, but you could also use pumpkin, cabbage, carrot and beans, depending on what you like.

Pour it over steamed rice with some fried vegetables on the side like Spicy Potato Fry (page 166) and Spicy Fried Eggplant (page 157).

Ingredients
Koottu spice blend
50 g (1.7 oz) desiccated or fresh grated coconut **(page 280)**
4 dried red chillies (adjust to taste)
1 teaspoon cumin seeds
60 ml (2 fl oz) warm water

220 g (7.7 oz) yellow moong dhal or red lentils, rinsed and drained
700 ml (1 ½ pints) water
1 bunch spinach, leaves and stems finely chopped
20 fresh curry leaves
¼ teaspoon turmeric powder
¼ teaspoon asafoetida
½ teaspoon salt
2 teaspoon ghee or canola oil
1 teaspoon black mustard seeds

continued over the page...

Method

Place all the ingredients for the koottu spice blend with 60 ml (2 oz) warm water into a spice grinder and process to a fine paste, adding extra warm water if needed.

Place lentils with 700 ml (1½ pints) of water in a large saucepan, cook over a medium-high heat, stirring occasionally. After 10 to 12 minutes the lentils should be half cooked, the lentil should be soft on the outside but firm on the inside, at this point add the chopped spinach, curry leaves, ground coconut paste, turmeric, asafoetida and salt. Stir well. Cook for another 10 minutes until the lentils are completely soft and the spinach is cooked. Remove from the heat.

In a small frying pan heat the ghee or oil over a medium heat, add mustard seeds when they start to pop quickly pour over the lentil spinach curry, mix well.

Mixed Lentil Dhal

Serves: 4–6 as part of a shared meal
Cooking Difficulty: Easy

Dhal is a staple in Indian cuisine, growing up in the south meant the ones I grew up with were light and delicately spiced, in contrast to the more buttery and richer dhals of the north. We usually make dhal quite thick, so it can be mashed up with rice or scooped up with chapatis.

This one has the benefit of added nutritional value because of the variety of dhal used. You could also easily turn this into a hearty soup by adding extra water and a few vegetables like carrots and potatoes. A dollop of yogurt or raita always makes a good addition as a side.

Ingredients
55 g (1.9 oz) yellow moong dhal
50 g (1.7 oz) red lentils
50 g (1.7 oz) channa dhal or yellow split peas
700 ml (1½ pints) water
½ teaspoon turmeric powder
2 tablespoons ghee
1½ teaspoons cumin seeds
1 medium tomato, diced
5 cm (2 in) piece ginger, finely chopped
1 clove garlic, finely chopped
1 fresh green chilli, finely chopped
1 teaspoon cilantro (coriander) powder
1 teaspoon salt
4 tablespoons fresh cilantro (coriander), leaves and stalks finely chopped
Juice of a lemon

Method

Place all the lentils in a large heavy-based saucepan, rinse them in running cold water then drain. Add 700 ml (1½ pints) of water and turmeric to the lentils, and cook on a medium heat for 10 to 15 minutes until moong dhal is soft and mushy, the channa dhal will be firmer. Remove from heat and set aside.

In another saucepan, heat the ghee on a medium-high heat. Add the cumin seeds, and allow them to slightly sizzle for 10 seconds. Add the chopped tomato, ginger, garlic, chilli and cilantro powder, stir for 30 seconds.

Add the cooked lentils and salt, stir well. Lower the heat and simmer for 10 minutes, until all the lentils are cooked and the dhal is thick and creamy, if it's too thin let it simmer away for longer to reduce, if it's too dry add some water. Stir occasionally.

To finish stir through cilantro leaves and lemon juice, taste for salt and adjust to your liking.

Pasi Payaru

(Green Mung Bean Dhal with Ginger)

Serves: 6–8 people as part of a full meal
Cooking Difficulty: Easy

A South Indian mung dhal, with a bit more warmth and heat from gentle and warming fennel and sambar powder. Eat with Jeera Pulao (page 206), Chapatis (page 178) and Spicy Potato Fry (page 166).

Ingredients
200 g (7 oz) whole green mung beans, soaked for an hour
700 ml (1½ pints) water
2 tablespoons ghee
2 teaspoons fennel seeds
5 cm (2 in) cube ginger, finely diced
10 curry leaves
½ teaspoon sambar powder **(page 285)**
¼ teaspoon turmeric powder
1 medium tomato, roughly chopped
½ teaspoon salt
4 tablespoons fresh cilantro (coriander), stalks and leaves finely chopped
Juice of half a lemon

Method

In a large saucepan cook the mung beans with 700 ml (1½ pints) of water until tender, it should take about 30 to 40 minutes. Remove from the heat and set aside.

Heat the ghee in a deep pan on medium-high, add the fennel seeds and stir for a few seconds. Add the ginger and curry leaves and stir for 30 seconds. Add the sambar and turmeric powder, stir for 10 seconds, then add the tomatoes and salt. Continue to stir together for a minute or so until the tomatoes soften and release their juice.

Add the cooked mung dhal, stir well. Add 240 ml (8 fl oz) of water to get a good thick soupy consistency, if too thick add a bit more water.

Lower the heat and simmer for 10 minutes. Remove from heat, and stir through cilantro leaves and lemon juice.

Pumpkin and Black-Eyed Peas Koottu

Serves: 4–6

Cooking Difficulty: Easy

This koottu uses black-eyed peas instead of red lentils to make a really hearty dish. If you add a bit more water you could eat it on its own as a soup, or you can eat it with steamed rice, Cauliflower Fry (page 156) and a bit of yogurt.

Ingredients

Koottu spice blend

50 g (1.7 oz) desiccated or fresh grated coconut **(page 280)**
4 dried red chillies (adjust to taste)
1 teaspoon cumin seeds
60 ml (2 fl oz) warm water

80 g (2.8 oz) black-eyed peas, soaked overnight or at least for 4 hours
950 ml (2 pints) water
240 g (8.4 oz) pumpkin, cut into 3 cm (1¼ in) cubes
20 fresh curry leaves
¼ teaspoon asafoetida
¼ teaspoon turmeric powder
½ teaspoon salt
2 teaspoons ghee or canola oil
1 teaspoon black mustard seeds
7 tablespoons chopped cilantro (coriander) leaves

continued over the page...

Method

Place all ingredients for the koottu spice blend with 60 ml (2 oz) of warm water into a spice grinder and process to a fine paste.

Place the black-eyed peas with 950 ml (2 pints) water in a large saucepan and cook on a medium to high heat for 20 to 30 minutes, until soft but still with a bit of bite.

Once the peas are cooked, add the pumpkin, ground coconut paste, curry leaves, asafoetida, turmeric powder and salt. Stir together and continue to cook for a further 5 to 10 minutes until the pumpkin is soft. Remove from the heat.

In a small frying pan heat the ghee or oil, add the mustard seeds, when they start to pop pour over the koottu, mix well. Garnish with the chopped cilantro leaves.

Sodhi
(Light Coconut Milk Curry)

Serves: 4
Cooking Difficulty: Easy

This is a traditional dish from my home town of Tirunelveli, a light coconut milk curry that's eaten with "iddiyapums" which are freshly made rice noodles, packet rice noodles make a good substitute.

Ingredients
2 red onions, thinly sliced
6 cloves garlic, thinly sliced
10 curry leaves
1 fresh green chilli, finely chopped
2 medium tomatoes, cut into quarters
¼ teaspoon turmeric powder
2 small potatoes cut into 2 cm (¾ in) pieces
1 carrot, cut into 2 cm (¾ in) pieces
15 green beans, cut into 2 cm (¾ in) pieces
240 ml (8 fl oz) water
1 teaspoon salt
220 ml (7.7 fl oz) coconut milk

Method
Heat the oil in a deep frying pan over a medium-high heat. Fry the onion, garlic and curry leaves for 2 minutes until the onion goes soft and translucent. Add the green chilli, tomatoes and turmeric powder continue to stir for few minutes until the tomatoes start to soften. Add the potatoes, carrots and beans, stir well. Add 240 ml (8 fl oz) water and salt, lower heat and simmer for 5 minutes or until vegetables are cooked but still firm. Finally add the coconut milk and simmer for 5 minutes. Taste for salt and adjust as needed.

Spoon over steamed rice or vermicelli.

Quick Cauliflower Kurma

Serves: 4 as part of a shared meal
Cooking Difficulty: Easy

This caulfilower kurma is a bit easier to make than the vegetable kurma as it uses coconut milk and dried spices instead of grinding a fresh paste. You could easily add other vegetables to this if you would like, peas, potatoes and carrots would all go well. It has a subtle and sweet flavor from the star anise and cilantro.

Eat with Chapatis (page 178), Puris (page 181) or your favorite Pulao.

Ingredients
3 tablespoons canola oil
3 bay leaves
1 whole star anise
1 large onion, finely chopped
5 cm (2 in) piece ginger, finely chopped
2 cloves garlic, finely chopped
1 small hot green chilli, finely chopped
½ teaspoon turmeric powder
½ teaspoon chilli powder
2 teaspoons cilantro (coriander) powder
2 tomatoes, roughly chopped
70 g (2.5 oz) cashews, finely ground
120 ml (4 fl oz) coconut milk
1 teaspoon salt
1 cauliflower, cut into small florets
350 ml (12 fl oz) water
Large handful cilantro (coriander), stalks and leaves chopped

continued over the page...

Method

Heat the oil in a large frying pan over a medium heat, add the bay leaves and star anise and stir for a few seconds. Add the onion, ginger, garlic and green chilli, cook until the onion is soft and translucent. Add the rest of the spices, stir for 30 seconds. Add chopped tomatoes, mix well and cook for 2 minutes until soft and reduced. Now add ground cashews, coconut milk and salt, stir well.

Add cauliflower, mix well and cook for a few minutes then pour in the water, stir. When the mixture starts to bubble give it another quick stir then, lower the heat cover with a lid and simmer for 10 to 15 minutes, stirring occasionally until the cauliflower is soft and tender. Garnish with chopped cilantro leaves.

Easy Sambar

Serves: 4–6 as part of a shared meal
Cooking Difficulty: Easy

This is an easy way to make sambar, in the one pot, and by using red lentils instead of toor dhal, it is much quicker. You can add extra vegetables, like carrots and potatoes, to make a heartier dhal, or eat in the traditional way spooned over rice with a side of vegetables.

Ingredients
For the sambar powder
3 teaspoons cilantro (coriander) seeds
½ teaspoon channa dhal or yellow split peas
½ teaspoon toor dhal
¼ teaspoon yellow mung dhal
¼ teaspoon turmeric powder
2 teaspoon hot chilli powder

1 tablespoon canola oil
1 teaspoon black mustard seeds
2 whole dried red chillies
1 medium red onion, roughly chopped
2 carrots, chopped in 2 cm (¾ in) pieces
1 red or green bell pepper (capsicum), chopped in 2 cm (¾ in) pieces
1 large tomato, roughly diced
10 curry leaves
200 g (7 oz) red lentils, rinsed and drained
6 tablespoons cilantro (coriander), stalks and leaves roughly chopped
1 teaspoon turmeric powder
1 teaspoon cumin powder
Pinch asafoetida
1 teaspoon salt
700 ml (1½ pints) water
½ large lemon

Method

For the sambar powder
Place a non-stick frying pan on a medium heat. Add the cilantro seeds and all the dhals and dry roast for 2 minutes, until fragrant. Transfer to a plate and allow to cool. Place your roasted ingredients along with the turmeric and chilli powder in a spice grinder and process to a fine powder.

Heat the oil in a large saucepan over a medium-high heat. Add the mustard seeds, when they start to pop add dried red chillies and stir for a few seconds. Turn the heat down slightly, then add the onion, chopped vegetables, tomatoes and curry leaves, stir for a minute. Add the red lentils, half the cilantro, all the spices and salt, stir until combined.

Add water, bring to the boil and then lower the heat to simmer for 20 minutes until lentils are soft, stir occasionally.

Finally, bring the mixture to the boil and allow to gently bubble away for a few more minutes, until you get a thicker consistency more like a stew than a soup.

Take the pan off the heat, and add the juice of half a lemon and remaining cilantro.

Rajma
(Creamy Kidney Beans)

Serves: 4–6
Cooking Difficulty: Easy

A popular dish in the north, this is a great way to use red kidney beans. Dried kidney beans will create a much nicer dish, but if you just want something quick tinned beans will do the job.

Ingredients
185 g (6.5 oz) dried red kidney beans, soaked overnight or 2 tins red kidney beans
820 ml (27.7 fl oz) water
2 tablespoons canola oil
1 large onion, finely diced
2.5 cm (1 in) piece ginger, finely chopped
2 cloves garlic, finely chopped
½ teaspoon cumin powder
1 teaspoon cilantro (coriander) powder
½ teaspoon garam masala (page 284)
¼ teaspoon turmeric powder
½ teaspoon chilli powder
2 tomatoes, diced
1 teaspoon salt
4 tablespoons cilantro (coriander) leaves

Method

Place the kidney beans in a small saucepan with water and cook for 30 minutes, until soft, adding more water to cook if it dries out.

Heat oil in a deep frying pan on a medium-high heat, add onion, ginger and garlic stir for 2 minutes or until the onion turns golden brown. Add all the spices and stir for a minute, then add the tomatoes and salt. Stir well and cook until the tomatoes break down and you get a thick paste.

Finally add the cooked kidney beans with an extra 120 ml (4 fl oz) of water, stir well. Lower the heat and simmer for 10 minutes, until it's thick and creamy.

Garnish with chopped cilantro leaves.

Simple Dhal

Serves: 4–6
Cooking Difficulty: Easy

My son thinks there's nothing quite as perfect as a good dhal, it's high in protein but low in fat, and when eaten with rice or Indian breads forms a complete protein source. That's probably why you can't help but feel good after eating it.

When it comes to cooking a good dhal, once you get the knack of preparing the right base (tempering spices in ghee, and adding sauteed onion, garlic, ginger, chilli and tomato) you can be as creative as you like with the kind of lentils you use and vegetables you add, and be certain you'll make something delicious every time.

Ingredients
200 g (7 oz) red lentils, soaked for 10 minutes
2 tablespoons ghee
1 teaspoon cumin seeds
1 red onion, finely diced
1 small hot green chilli (adjust to taste)
2.5 cm (1 in) ginger, finely diced
1 teaspoon cumin powder
1 teaspoon cilantro (coriander) powder
¼ teaspoon turmeric powder
¼ teaspoon chilli powder (adjust to taste)
Pinch of asafoetida
1 medium tomato, roughly chopped
½ teaspoon salt
475 ml (16 fl oz) water
Handful cilantro (coriander), stalks and leaves roughly chopped
Juice of a lemon

Method

Heat ghee, or oil, in a heavy based saucepan on a medium heat. Add cumin seeds, and allow them to slightly sizzle. Then add the onions, green chilli and ginger, stir until the onion is soft and translucent. Add all of the spices, stir well.

Add the chopped tomatoes, salt and drained lentils, stir well to coat everything in the spices. Add 475 ml (16 fl oz) water, stir well, then bring to the boil. Lower the heat and simmer for 15 minutes, until dhal is soft and mushy. Stir several times to ensure the dhal doesn't boil over or dry up, if you need to add more water add a little bit at a time.

To finish stir through cilantro leaves and lemon juice, taste for salt and adjust to your liking. Serve with rice, chapatis or parathas and your favorite vegetables.

Special Curries

Matar Paneer
(Green Peas and Ricotta in Gravy)

Serves: 4–6
Cooking Difficulty: Easy

A popular Indian dish from the north, spicy tomatoes with bursts of fresh peas and creamy paneer. It's a comforting dish, perfect when poured over any fluffy pulao or mopped up with Parathas (page 170) or Chapatis (page 178).

If you have time have a go at making your own Paneer (page 277), it will taste even better.

Ingredients
3 tablespoons ghee
1 medium red onion, finely diced
1 clove garlic, finely diced
2.5 cm (1 in) piece ginger, finely diced
1 tablespoon cumin powder
1 teaspoon garam masala **(page 284)**
1 teaspoon dried methi leaves (dried fenugreek leaves available in Indian stores)
½ teaspoon turmeric powder
½ teaspoon chilli powder
½ teaspoon salt
2 large ripe red tomatoes, roughly chopped
120 ml (4 fl oz) water
400 g (14 oz) paneer (home made page 277 or bought at the Indian store), cut into 2.5 cm (1 in) cubes
100 g (3.5 oz) peas, fresh or frozen
4 tablespoons cilantro (coriander), stalks and leaves roughly chopped

continued over the page...

Method

Heat ghee in a deep frying pan on medium-high heat. Add the onion, garlic and ginger, and stir until the onion turns slightly brown. Add all the spices and salt, stirring for a minute so the spices release their aroma and form a paste.

Add the chopped tomatoes, stir well and then cook for 2 minutes until the tomatoes are soft and mushy. Pour 120 ml (4 fl oz) water and cover with a lid. Reduce the heat and simmer for five minutes until the tomatoes reduce and thicken.

Add the chopped paneer and peas and cook on low heat for another 5 minutes with the lid on. Garnish with cilantro leaves.

Thakali Rasam

(Spicy Tomato and Tamarind Soup)

Serves: 4 as part of a shared meal
Cooking Difficulty: Medium

Rasam is the other ubiquitous curry, Sambar (page 131) being the other one, that's eaten almost everyday in south India. There are many varieties of Rasam from garlic (page 72) to pineapple but Thakali (tomato) Rasam is the most common one that you'll find. It's a balance of sour tamarind, tomatoes and freshly ground cumin, cilantro, pepper and chilli.

Eat with vegetables on the side like Cabbage Thoran (page 164) and some fried pappadums on the side.

Ingredients
Rasam Powder
2 teaspoons cilantro (coriander) seeds
2 teaspoons cumin seeds
2 dried chillies
¼ teaspoon pepper

1 tablespoon dried tamarind or 1 teaspoon tamarind paste
700 ml (1½ pints) water
2 ripe tomatoes, chopped into quarters
¼ teaspoon turmeric powder
½ teaspoon salt
15 curry leaves, roughly torn
¼ teaspoon asafoetida
4 tablespoons cilantro (coriander), leaves and stems finely chopped
1 teaspoon ghee
½ teaspoon black mustard seeds

continued over the page...

Method

To make the rasam powder, place all ingredients in a spice grinder and process to a coarse powder. Set aside.

Soak the dried tamarind in 240 ml (8 fl oz) of warm to hot water for 10 minutes. Squeeze the softened tamarind with your hand and mix the fibres with the water, strain through a fine sieve pushing as much pulp as you can through, set aside. If you're using tamarind paste simply stir it with 240 ml (8 fl oz) warm water and set aside.

In a small saucepan, mix the tomatoes, turmeric, salt, curry leaves, asafoetida and tamarind juice with 700 ml (1½ pints) of water. Place the saucepan on a medium high heat and allow to cook for 10 minutes, until tomatoes are soft. Use the back of a spoon crush half the tomatoes a little, then add 1 tablespoon of rasam powder, cilantro and 120 ml (4 fl oz) of water, stir well.

Immediately turn the heat down on the lowest setting and simmer for 5 minutes. If it starts bubbling turn the heat down lower or move to a smaller burner. After a few minutes an orangey froth will start to form on the top. Once the majority of the surface is covered with this froth, turn off the heat.

Heat ghee in a small pan, add mustard seeds and when they start to pop pour over rasam. This adds a nutty flavor and fragrance to this delicate thin soup.

Vegetable Kurma

Serves: 4–6 as part of shared meal
Cooking Difficulty: Medium

Kurma is a way of braising vegetables or meat in a rich paste of coconut, nuts and sometimes yogurt. Being South Indian we cooked our kurma with coconut and cashews rather than yogurt or cream, the result is a lighter kurma with natural sweetness from the coconut.

Serve with Biryani (page 211), your favorite Pulao or with Fried Purls (page 181).

Ingredients
For the kurma paste
100 g (3.4 oz) desiccated or fresh grated coconut **(page 280)**
70 g (2.5 oz) cashews
4 dried chillies (adjust according to taste)
3 cloves garlic, finely sliced
5 cm (2 in) piece ginger, finely sliced
1 teaspoon garam masala **(page 284)**
¼ teaspoon fennel seeds
½ teaspoon turmeric powder
80 ml (3 fl oz) warm water

3 tablespoons canola oil
2 red onions, finely diced
1 large tomato, roughly chopped
475 ml (1 pint) water
2 potatoes, cut into 2 cm (¾ in) cubes
1 carrot, cut into 2 cm (¾ in) cubes
60 g (2.1 oz) peas, fresh or frozen
15 green beans, cut into 2 cm (¾ in) pieces
1 red bell pepper (capsicum), cut into 2 cm (¾ in) pieces
1 ½ teaspoon salt
4 tablespoons cilantro (coriander) leaves, chopped

Method

Place all ingredients for the kurma paste with warm water in a spice grinder and process into a paste.

Heat the oil in a deep frying pan on medium-high heat, add the onion and cook until lightly brown. Add the kurma paste, stir well and cook with the onions for 2 minutes. Add the tomatoes and cook until soft, then add 60 ml (2 fl oz) of water, stir well then lower the heat and cook for about 3 minutes to get a pale orange paste.

Increase the heat to medium, add all the vegetables and stir to combine well. Add the remaining water and salt, stir well. Bring the kurma to a bubble, lower the heat cover with a lid and cook for 15 to 20 minutes until the vegetables are tender. Stir occasionally to check consistency, if the kurma is too dry add a bit more water, it should have the consistency of a thick gravy.

Stir through cilantro.

Raji's Paneer Kofta Curry

Serves: 4–6 as part of a shared meal
Cooking Difficulty: Medium

My Dad's emphasis on good health and ayurveda, meant I didn't eat much spicy street food or go to restaurants to try the rich curries from the north. So when I left home I was excited to eat whatever I pleased, but I soon found myself modifying traditional northern recipes to make them a bit less creamy and rich.

This recipe was inspired by Malai Kofta, where ricotta, potato and spices are rolled into balls and deep fried then added to a creamy tomato sauce. I always found the kofta balls a bit too heavy, so decided to use good quality ricotta and a light blend of spices to make pan-fried ricotta patties instead.

After the first time I made it, I knew I was on to a winner, the kids lapped it up and sure enough when I served it at my next dinner party it was completely polished off.

Ingredients
For the koftas
200 g full-fat ricotta cheese, fresh from the deli*
2 tablespoons plain flour
1 teaspoon cumin powder
½ teaspoon salt
¼ teaspoons turmeric powder
1 tablespoon cilantro (coriander), leaves and stalks finely chopped
4 tablespoons ghee or oil for shallow frying koftas

Creamy Sauce
3 tablespoons canola oil
1 medium red onion, finely diced
1 clove garlic, finely grated
2cm (0.7 in) cube of ginger, peeled and finely grated
1 tablespoon cumin powder
2 teaspoons garam masala
½ teaspoon turmeric powder
½ teaspoon chilli powder
4 large tomatoes, diced or 400 g tin chopped tomatoes
½ teaspoon salt
100 ml (3.3 fl oz) cream
4 tablespoons cilantro (coriander), leaves and stalks finely chopped

*make sure to buy the ricotta from the supermarket deli or if you're buying it in a packet make sure it's one that has been set in a basket. The ricotta that comes in a tub has a higher water content and will be too wet to form patties.

Method
Making the ricotta koftas
In a large mixing bowl combine all the kofta ingredients, except the oil, and mix gently until well combined.

Take a tablespoon of the mixture and, using your hands, make a small round disc about 1 cm (½ in) thick and 5 cm (2 in) diameter. Place on a lightly floured plate. If the mixture becomes too sticky, coat your hands with plain flour. Continue this process until all the mixture has been used, you should get about 10 to 15 patties. Cover the plate with plastic wrap and set in the fridge for at least 10 minutes.

Once the patties are firm, remove from the fridge. Heat a few tablespoons of oil in a large non stick frying pan on medium heat. When the oil is hot, gently place patties on the pan, leaving enough room in between to turn over. Cook the patties for a few minutes on each side until they're golden brown. Dry on a plate with paper towel, refresh pan with a bit more oil between each batch of patties.

continued over the page...

For the creamy tomato sauce

Heat oil in a large deep frying pan on a medium heat. Once hot, add onion, garlic and ginger. Stir until the onion turns slightly brown. Then add all the spices, stir well. Add the chopped tomatoes, 120 ml (4 fl oz) water and salt, stir well. Cover with a lid, turn the heat to low and simmer for 5 minutes.

Stir in the cream and simmer for a couple of minutes with the lid off. Take the pan off the heat. If you're happy with a chunky sauce leave as is, if you prefer something smoother pour into a blender and process until smooth.

Pour the sauce into a serving bowl and gently place the cooked patties in the sauce, garnish with cilantro leaves.

Serve with fluffy Jeera Pulao **(page 206)** and Cucumber Raita **(page 240)**.

Avial

(Root Vegetable and Coconut Stew)

Serves: 4–6
Cooking Difficulty: Easy

Avial is a dish that hails from Kerela where it forms a common part of their diet. A Kerela style avial is a bit different to the Tamil one, with the addition of yogurt that makes it a bit wetter. The Tamil version that I've shared with you here, is a bit drier and eaten as a vegetable dish on the side when we eat Rasam (page 105) or Sambar (page 131) with rice.

If you do want more of a gravy, add 120 g (4.5 oz) of yogurt when you add the coconut spice blend, and extra water when cooking the vegetables.

Ingredients
100 g (3.4 oz) desiccated or fresh grated coconut **(page 280)**
1 teaspoon cumin seeds
3 small hot green chillies

2 medium potatoes, washed and peeled
15 green beans, diagonally cut into 5 cm (2 in) slices
1 large carrot
1 green raw banana (plantain)
2 small lebanese eggplants (aubergines)
2 zucchinis (courgettes)
240 ml (8 fl oz) water
¼ teaspoon turmeric powder
1 teaspoon salt
20 curry leaves
2 tablespoons coconut oil

continued over the page...

Method

Place the coconut, cumin seeds and green chillies with 60 ml (2 fl oz) of warm water in a spice grinder and process to a smooth paste, adding extra water as needed.

Cut all the vegetables into thick matchsticks about 5 cm (2 in) long and 1 cm (½ in) thick, keeping each vegetable separate.

To accommodate even cooking of the vegetables, place them in a 2 litre (4 pints) saucepan in the following order: potatoes, beans, carrots, green raw bananas, eggplant and zucchinis. Sprinkle with the turmeric powder and salt then pour 240 ml (8 fl oz) of water to cover everything.

Place on medium-high heat, cover with a lid and cook for 5 minutes, until vegetables are half cooked. Add the ground coconut paste and curry leaves, stir well. Lower the heat and cook for 2 minutes, until the vegetables are cooked, but not too soft. Remove the lid and simmer for 2 minutes, evaporating any excess water. Finish by stirring through coconut oil.

North Indian Green Mung Bean Dhal

Serves: 4–6 as part of a shared meal
Cooking Difficulty: Medium

A simple mung dhal drawing on the flavors of north India featuring garam masala and fragrant methi leaves. Eat with rice or Chapatis (page 178) and a dollop of yogurt, for a comforting meal.

Ingredients
130 g (4.6 oz) whole green mung dhal, soaked for 2 hours
2 tablespoons canola oil
1 red onion, roughly chopped
2 cloves garlic, finely grated
2.5 cm (1 in) piece ginger, finely grated
1 small hot green chilli
1 teaspoon garam masala **(page 284)**
½ teaspoon cilantro (coriander) powder
½ teaspoon turmeric
½ teaspoon cumin powder
¼ teaspoon chilli powder
2 tomatoes, roughly chopped
1 teaspoon salt
1 teaspoon methi leaves (dried fenugreek leaves available at Indian stores)

Method

Place the mung beans with 475 ml (2 pints) of water in a small saucepan on a medium heat. Gently boil for 20 to 30 minutes until the mung beans are tender, stir occasionally. Once cooked, take off the heat and set aside.

Heat the oil in a large heavy based saucepan on a medium heat. Add the onions, garlic, ginger and green chilli, stir until the onion is soft and translucent. Add all the spices and stir well.

Add the chopped tomatoes, salt and 60 ml (2 fl oz) of water, stir well. Allow the tomatoes to cook until completely soft, then crush slightly using a potato masher. Stir through the methi leaves.

Finally add the cooked mung dhal and another 360 ml (10 fl oz) of water. Simmer for 10 minutes until you have a nice thick dhal, if it's too dry add more water and if it's too thin allow it to bubble away until it reduces.

Garnish with cilantro.

Pakora Khadi
(Besan Fritters in Rich Yogurt Sauce)

Serves: 4–6
Cooking Difficulty: Medium

Besan flour gets used in two key ways to make this thick sour creamy dish: to make pakoras and also dry roasted and incorporated into the curry itself. The ingredients used might seem a few too many, but if you give it a try you'll be rewarded with a curry like no other.

This dish will wow guests and is definitely complete enough to serve on it's own just with some Jeera Pulao (page 206) or a few Chapatis (page 178) to mop everything up with.

Ingredients
For the fritters
Canola oil for deep frying
196 g (6.8 oz) besan flour (chickpea flour available at Indian grocery stores)
½ red onion, finely diced
1 green chilli, finely chopped
Salt to taste
120 ml (4 fl oz) water

For the yogurt sauce
65 g (2.2 oz) besan flour
350 ml (12 fl oz) natural yogurt
700 ml (1 ½ pints) water

Spices for the sauce
1 teaspoon mustard seeds
1 tablespoon cilantro (coriander) seeds, coarsely pounded
4 dried red chillies, torn in half (adjust to taste)
1 large onion, diced
2 garlic cloves, finely chopped
5 cm (2 in) piece ginger, finely chopped
1 green chilli
15 curry leaves

Pinch of asafoetida
1 teaspoon garam masala **(page 284)**
1 teaspoon turmeric powder
1 teaspoon salt
2 medium tomatoes, roughly chopped
2 teaspoons dried methi leaves (dried fenugreek leaves available in Indian stores)

Method

For the fritters
Fill a deep frying pan two thirds full with canola oil, heat on a medium-high heat. While oil is getting hot, mix besan, onion, chilli and salt in a large bowl. While mixing, slowly pour in 120 ml (4 fl oz) of water to make a thick batter.

To test if the oil is the right temperature, drop a tiny bit of batter into the oil, if the batter bubbles and rises to the top it's just right, if the batter sinks to the bottom wait until the oil gets hotter; if it burns and smokes it's too hot, reduce the heat.

Use your hand to scoop a tablespoon of batter and carefully drop it into oil. Cook about 5 to 6 pakoras at a time, turning occasionally and cook until golden brown. Use a slotted spoon to scoop them out and drain on paper towel. Repeat with the remaining batter.

For the yogurt sauce
Heat a deep frying pan over a medium heat, and dry roast the besan for about 2 minutes, constantly stirring. Transfer to a plate to cool.

In a large mixing bowl pour the yogurt, water, toasted besan, a pinch of the turmeric powder and ½ teaspoon of the salt. Gently whisk together until smooth. Set aside for 15 minutes.

Heat the oil in a deep frying pan over a medium-high heat, add mustard seeds when they start to pop add crushed cilantro seeds and dry red chillies. Stir for a minute to toast the spices and then add the onions and cook until soft. Add garlic, ginger, green chillies, curry leaves and asafoetida, stir for a minute. Add garam masala, turmeric powder and salt, cook for a minute. Add the tomatoes and cook until soft and they release their juices. Lastly, add the yogurt mixture, stir until smooth. Lower the heat and simmer for 10 minutes, stirring occasionally. Add the methi leaves by crushing them between your palms over the gravy. Gently drop in the cooked pakoras, mix well. Cook on a low heat for another 5 minutes, so the pakoras soak up the lovely curry.

Morkuzhambu

(Spicy Buttermilk Curry)

Serves: 4–6
Cooking Difficulty: Easy

Buttermilk is the key ingredient in this dish, and combined with a bit of chilli and cumin seeds makes a sour and slightly spicy curry. Traditionally we add winter melon to this curry, but as an alternative I have added fried eggplant instead which adds a nice texture.

Fluffy steamed rice or Adai (page 224) make the perfect accompaniments.

Ingredients
2 baby eggplants (aubergines), cut into 2 cm (¾ in) cubes
2 tablespoons canola oil
100 g (3.5 oz) desiccated or fresh grated coconut **(page 280)**
4 dried chillies
1 teaspoon cumin seeds
¼ teaspoon turmeric powder
240 ml (8 fl oz) thick greek style yogurt
240 ml (8 fl oz) buttermilk
120 ml (4 fl oz) water
1 teaspoon salt
1 teaspoon canola oil
1 teaspoon black mustard seeds
15 curry leaves
4 tablespoons chopped cilantro (coriander) leaves

continued over the page...

Method

Heat oil in a frying pan on medium-high heat and cook the eggplant with a small sprinkle of salt for 5 minutes until eggplant is cooked through. Remove from the heat and set aside.

Place the coconut, chillies, cumin seeds and turmeric powder with 80 ml (3 fl oz) of warm water in a spice grinder and process to a fine paste, add more water as needed. In a large bowl add the yogurt, buttermilk, water, ground coconut paste and salt, whisk together.

Heat the oil in a deep frying pan on medium-high heat, add the mustard seeds and when they start to pop add curry leaves stir for 10 seconds, then add the cooked eggplant and yogurt mix. Immediately lower the heat, stir well.

Simmer gently for about 2 minutes, continually stirring. When you see tiny bubbles or froth appear on the surface, immediately turn off the heat, be careful not to break the boil as the mixture will curdle.

Add the cilantro leaves, stir and transfer to a serving dish.

If you have leftovers, you could try using this gravy as a salad dressing or drizzled over roasted vegetables. If reheating to eat the next day, gently heat on the stove on low heat for a minute without breaking the boil, don't use the microwave as it will curdle.

Theeyal
(Tamarind Curry with Fried Onion and Coconut)

Serves: 4–6
Cooking Difficulty: Easy

This was another dish that my Mum learnt from a neighbour, it's similar to some Tamil dishes that use a lot of tamarind to make a thick chilli curry that we spoon over rice. It also tastes particularly nice eaten with Coconut Rice (page 190).

This recipe is for the basic version of theeyal and doesn't include any vegetables, but you could add some okra, eggplant or zucchini after the onions have fried if you wanted a bit more to it. As it's from a coastal town there's also some non-hindu versions of the dish that use fish, which you could poach in the curry once it's done. Serve with fluffy steamed rice and any kind of vegetables.

Ingredients
2 tablespoons firmly packed dried tamarind or 2 teaspoons tamarind paste
240 ml (8 fl oz) warm water
100 g (3.5 oz) desiccated or fresh grated coconut **(page 280)**
2 tablespoons cilantro (coriander) seeds
4–6 dried chillies (adjust to taste)
120 ml (4 fl oz) warm water
3 tablespoons canola oil
500 g (17.5 oz) small red pearl onions or shallots, peeled and finely sliced
25 curry leaves
¼ teaspoon turmeric powder
1 teaspoon salt
475 ml (1 pint) water

Method

Soak the dried tamarind in 240 ml (8 fl oz) of warm to hot water for 10 minutes. Squeeze the softened tamarind with your hand and mix the fibres well in the water, strain through a fine sieve pushing as much pulp as you can through, set aside. If you're using tamarind paste simply stir it with 240 ml (8 fl oz) warm water and set aside.

Heat a frying pan on medium-high heat and toast the coconut for 2 minutes, stirring so the coconut doesn't burn. Add the cilantro seeds and chillies and continue to stir until coconut lightly browns. Transfer to a plate to cool. Place in a spice blender with 120 ml (4 fl oz) warm water and process into a paste.

Heat the oil in a deep frying pan on medium-high heat, add onions and cook until golden brown. Add the coconut paste, curry leaves, turmeric powder and salt, stir and cook for 2 minutes. Add tamarind liquid and 475 ml (1 pint) of water. Mix well, bring to a boil, then reduce heat and simmer for 15 minutes until it's reduced and quite thick.

Wait for the curry to cool a little before eating with brown rice and a few dollops of ghee. Crunchy green beans are a perfect side for this dish. It tastes even better the next day.

Pulikuzhambu
(South Indian Tamarind Chilli Curry)

Serves: 4–6 as part of a shared meal
Cooking Difficulty: Medium

A popular curry in Tamilnadu, eaten by people from all backgrounds. Hindus add eggplant and drumsticks, non-Hindus add fish and shellfish, add whatever you enjoy most.

It definitely tastes better, and spicier, the next day when the flavors have developed. Eat with nutty brown rice with a bit of ghee drizzled on top, accompanied by fresh Beans or Cabbage Thoran (page 164) is just perfect.

Ingredients
For Sambar powder:
3 teaspoons cilantro (coriander) seeds
½ teaspoon channa dhal or yellow split peas
½ teaspoon toor dhal
¼ teaspoon yellow mung dhal
¼ teaspoon turmeric powder
2 teaspoon hot chilli powder

Pulikuzhambu
2 tablespoons firmly packed dried tamarind or 2 teaspoons tamarind paste
240 ml (8 fl oz) warm water
2 tablespoon canola oil
1 teaspoon black mustard seeds
Pinch asafoetida
2 red onion, roughly diced
15 fresh curry leaves
2 tablespoons sambar powder **(see above)**
1 tomato, roughly chopped
475 ml (1 pint) water
1 teaspoon salt
6 tablespoons cilantro (coriander), stalks and leaves roughly chopped

Method

For the sambar powder

Place a non-stick frying pan on a medium heat. Add the cilantro seeds and all the dhals and dry roast for 2 minutes, until fragrant. Transfer to a plate and allow to cool. Place your roasted ingredients along with the turmeric and chilli powder in a spice grinder and process to a fine powder.

For the Pulikuzhambu

Soak the dried tamarind in 240 ml (8 fl oz) of warm to hot water for 10 minutes. Squeeze the softened tamarind with your hand and mix the fibres well in the water, strain through a fine sieve pushing as much pulp as you can through, set aside. If you're using tamarind paste simply stir that with 240 ml (8 fl oz) of warm water and set aside.

Heat oil in a large frying pan on a medium heat. Add the mustard seeds, when they start to pop add the asafoetida, stir for a few seconds. Add the onion and curry leaves, stir for 2 minutes or until onion starts to become translucent. Add the sambar powder, 60 ml (2 fl oz) water and continue to cook for a minute. Now add the tamarind juice, tomatoes, 475 ml (1 pint) water and salt, stir well.

Bring to the boil then lower the heat, cover with a lid and simmer for 10 minutes, stirring occasionally. Remove the lid, turn the heat up a little and allow to bubble away for 5 minutes or until you get a nice thick gravy consistency. Garnish with cilantro.

Sambar

(South Indian Sour and Spicy Dhal)

Serves: 4–6 as part of a shared meal
Cooking Difficulty: Medium

Tamils could eat Sambar for breakfast lunch or dinner, in fact they sometimes do! For breakfast it's served on the side to dip crispy hot Dosai (page 218) or Masala Vada (page 41), for lunch it's eaten with rice and vegetables and for dinner you could have the same again.

It's the toor dhal that really gives this dish the right creamy consistency so although it takes a bit of time to prepare, it's well worth it. You can also try using different vegetables in this dish like eggplant, turnips, pumpkin, squash and carrot, instead of bell pepper.

Ingredients
For Sambar powder:
3 teaspoons cilantro (coriander) seeds
½ teaspoon channa dhal or yellow split peas
½ teaspoon toor dhal
¼ teaspoon yellow moong dhal
¼ teaspoon turmeric powder
2 teaspoons hot chilli powder

1 tablespoon firmly packed dried tamarind or 2 teaspoons tamarind paste
240 ml (8 fl oz) warm water
200 g (7 oz) toor dhal, soaked overnight
475 ml (1 pint) water
1 tablespoon canola oil
1 teaspoon black mustard seeds
2 whole dried red chillies
Pinch asafoetida
1 red onion, roughly diced
1 red or green bell pepper (capsicum), chopped in 2 cm (¾ in) chunks
10 fresh curry leaves
1 medium tomato, roughly chopped

2 tablespoons sambar powder **(page 131)**
1 teaspoon turmeric powder
1 teaspoon salt
240 ml (8 fl oz) water
20g (¾ oz) cilantro (coriander), stalks and leaves roughly chopped

Method

For the sambar powder
Place a non-stick frying pan on a medium heat. Add cilantro seeds and all the dhals and dry roast for 2 minutes, until fragrant. Transfer to a plate and allow to cool. Place your roasted ingredients along with turmeric and chilli powder in a spice grinder and process to a fine powder.

For the Sambar
Soak dried tamarind in 240 ml (8 fl oz) of warm to hot water for 10 minutes. Squeeze the softened tamarind with your hand and mix the fibres well in the water, strain through a fine sieve pushing as much pulp as you can through, set aside. If you're using tamarind paste simply stir that with 240 ml (8 fl oz) warm water and set aside.

Place the toor dal, ¼ teaspoon turmeric and a pinch of asafoetida with 475 ml (1 pint) of water in a large saucepan. Cook on a medium heat, stirring frequently. Once the water has reduced by half cover with a lid and cook until lentils are soft and mushy. Set aside.

Heat the oil in a large frying pan on a medium heat. Add the mustard seeds, when they start to pop add the dried chilli and asafetida, stir for a few seconds. Add onion, bell pepper and curry leaves, stir for 30 seconds. Add the tamarind water, tomatoes, turmeric, sambar powder and salt, stir well. Bring to the boil and then simmer with the lid on for 5 minutes.

Add 240 ml (8 fl oz) of water to the cooked toor dhal and mix well. Add this to the tamarind base and stir. Taste, if you would like more spice add extra sambar powder.

Bring to a gentle boil, turn the heat down slightly and then allow the sambar to gently simmer for 5 minutes.

Once a froth forms on the top turn the heat off and garnish with fresh cilantro.

Palak Paneer

(Spicy Spinach with Indian Ricotta)

Serves: 4–6
Cooking Difficulty: Medium

This is another popular dish in the north, and is a nice way to use leafy green vegetables when they're in abundance. English spinach is what I commonly use but you can also go for swiss chard or silverbeet, if you're using one of those varieties discard the stalks and just use the green leaves.

Ingredients:
2 tablespoons canola oil
2 bunches English spinach or 1 bunch silverbeet, washed and finely chopped
2 small hot green chillies, finely chopped (adjust to taste)
2.5 cm (1 in) piece ginger, finely chopped
175 ml (6 fl oz) water
1 large onion, finely chopped
1 clove garlic, finely chopped
¼ teaspoon turmeric powder
1 teaspoon garam masala **(page 284)**
½ teaspoon cilantro (coriander) powder
1 teaspoon cumin powder
¼ teaspoon chilli powder
1 teaspoon salt
2 medium ripe tomatoes, diced
400 g (14 oz) paneer, (home made **page 277** or bought at the Indian store),
cut into 2.5 cm (1 in) cubes
1 tablespoon ghee

Method:

Heat 1 tablespoon of oil in a frying pan over a medium heat. When the oil is hot, add the spinach, green chillies and half the ginger, stir well until the spinach is wilted. Add 120 ml (4 fl oz) of water and cook until the spinach is completely soft. Transfer to a bowl.

Quickly rinse and dry the pan, and place it back on heat. Add 1 tablespoon of oil, when hot add the onion, the remaing ginger and the garlic, stirring until the onion is soft and translucent. Add all the dried spices and salt, stir for 20 seconds, then add the tomatoes, mix well. Add 60 ml (2 fl oz) of water, stir and lower the heat cooking for 2 minutes until tomatoes have reduced and formed a thick gravy.

While the tomatoes are cooking, blend the spinach until smooth using a hand-held blender or food processor. Add the spinach to the cooked tomato mix, stir well. Taste for salt and adjust to taste. Place paneer cubes in the spinach curry and gently stir through. Add ghee and simmer for 3 to 4 minutes, until paneer is lovely and soft and completely incorporated in the spinach.

Vegetables

Beans Usili

(Steamed Green Beans and Yellow Lentils)

Serves: 4–6 as part of a shared meal
Cooking Difficulty: Medium

Channa dhal is soaked, ground and steamed to make a delicious crumb that's stirred through beans. This is a very traditional Tamil brahmin dish and it's my favorite way to cook beans. It's so tasty that you could eat a whole bowl of them on their own, or just pile up some on the side with Rasam (page 105) or Sambar (page 131) with rice. You can also try cauliflower or broccoli instead of beans.

Ingredients
65 g (2.2 oz) channa dhal or yellow split peas, soaked for 20 minutes
400 g (14 oz) fresh green beans, cut into small pieces
3 dried red chillies (adjust to taste)
¼ teaspoon turmeric powder
¾ teaspoon salt
Pinch of asafoetida
1 tablespoon canola oil
½ teaspoon black mustard seeds
½ teaspoon urad dhal
15 fresh curry leaves

continued over the page...

Method

Add 475 ml (1 pint) of water to a large saucepan and bring to the boil, add diced beans with ½ teaspoon salt and cook for 2 to 3 minutes until just tender. Drain and set aside.

Place channa dhal, red chillies, turmeric, ¼ teaspoon of the salt and asafoetida with 1 tablespoon of water in a blender and process until you get a dry coarse mixture. Divide the mixture into 4 to 5 round patties and set aside.

Place a steamer in a pot with water and bring to the boil. Place the ground dhal patties in the steamer for 10 minutes. To check if they're cooked slide a toothpick through the patties if it slides out cleanly, then the channa dhal is cooked. Transfer to a plate and cool, then using your fingers break up the patties to a chunky crumb.

Heat oil in a large non-stick frying pan on medium-high heat. Add the mustard seeds, when they start to pop add the urad dhal, stir until slightly brown. Add the crumbed dhal mixture, boiled beans, curry leaves and stir well. Lower the heat and cook for 3 to 4 minutes, until everything is well combined and the crumb slightly browns.

Bindi Masala

(Dry Fried Okra in North Indian Spices)

Serves: 4–6
Cooking Difficulty: Easy

This is a really simple way to cook okra, but I think it really draws out the flavor. If you wanted a more substantial dish you could add potatoes, just cut them into thick matchsticks and cook with the okra.

This is a great vegetable to eat with Chapatis (page 178), Parathas (page 170) or your favorite Pulao.

Ingredients
500 g (17.5 oz) okra
3 tablespoon canola oil
¼ teaspoon cumin seeds
1 medium onion, thinly sliced
½ teaspoon garam masala **(page 284)**
¼ teaspoon turmeric powder
¼ teaspoon chilli powder
¼ teaspoon salt
2 tablespoons cilantro (coriander), stalks and leaves roughly chopped

Method
Wash the okra and pat dry with paper towel. Slice okra diagonally into 4 cm (1½ in) pieces.

Heat oil in a large non-stick frying pan on medium to high heat. Add cumin seeds, and allow them to slightly sizzle. Add the onion and cook until soft and slightly brown. Add all spices and salt, stir for a minute. Add the okra, stir well.

Lower the heat and cover the pan, keeping the lid slightly ajar to release steam. Cook until the okra is soft, stirring occasionally. Then remove the lid, turn the heat up a little and cook until the okra is slightly brown and crispy.

Enai Kathirikkai

(Baby Eggplants Stuffed with Spices)

Serves: 4 as part of a shared meal
Cooking Difficulty: Medium

Every vegetable has it's own flavor and texture, my Dad taught us to honour that and cook in a way that reflected each vegetables flavor, rather than drowning it out in too much spice. In my opinion this is the perfect way to use small baby eggplants, the kind we get in India are small and round and have a pale streaky skin. Stuffing this with a simple blend of channa dhal and spices gives just the right amount of flavor.

Serve on the side when eating Rasam (page 105) or Sambar (page 131) and rice. Lemon Rice (page 192) also makes a wonderful combination.

Ingredients
10–12 baby eggplants (aubergines)
50 g (1.7 oz) channa dhal or yellow split peas
1 tablespoon cilantro (coriander) seeds
3–4 dried red chillies
¼ teaspoon turmeric powder
60 ml (2 fl oz) water
1 teaspoon salt
4 tablespoons canola oil (canola or sunflower)
2 stalks curry leaves

Method:
Place the channa dhal and cilantro seeds in a heavy-based frying pan over a medium-high heat. Stir until channa dhal is toasted and starts to turn golden brown. Then add dried chillies and stir for another 30 seconds. Remove from heat.

Place the toasted spices, turmeric and 60 ml (2 fl oz) water in a spice grinder and process into a coarse paste. Adding more water if it's too dry.

Wash and pat dry the eggplant. Make a long cut lengthwise through each eggplant 1 cm (½ in) from the top, so each one has a long slit and it's top still on.

144

Rub eggplants with salt then gently stuff 1 to 2 teaspoons of the ground spice mix in the slit. Repeat for all the eggplants. Place on a tray and refrigerate for at least 30 minutes, you can also prepare the day before and marinate overnight.

Heat oil over a medium heat in a large heavy-based frying pan. Place the marinated eggplants so they sit side by side in the pan, don't stack them on top of each other as they won't cook properly. Stir through the curry leaves and gently stir the eggplants to ensure they are well coated with the oil.

Cover the pan and cook for 10 minutes, turning the eggplants over a few times so they cook evenly and their skins gets blistered on all sides. Once the eggplants are soft but still tender remove the lid and cook for another 5 minutes, again turning the eggplants over a few times.

The eggplants should be perfectly soft by now, and ready to be eaten. Allow to cool slightly before eating.

Masala Potato

(Turmeric and Ginger Potatoes)

Serves: 4–6 as part of a shared meal
Cooking Difficulty: Easy

My daughter's friend always asks me to make 'yellow potato' which is a simple way to describe this South Indian potato dish. The ginger is what really stands out in this dish, and the way you cook it makes it really creamy.

It perfectly accompanies Puris (page 181) or the famous Masala Dosai (page 220).

Ingredients
4 large potatoes
2 tablespoons canola oil
1 teaspoon black mustard seeds
1 teaspoon urad dhal
1 teaspoon channa dhal or yellow split peas
1 red onion, finely diced
5 cm (2 in) piece ginger, finely diced
1 small hot green chilli, finely diced
15 curry leaves, roughly torn
½ teaspoon turmeric powder
½ teaspoon salt
Pinch of asafoetida
240 ml (8 fl oz) water
4 tablespoons cilantro (coriander), finely chopped

continued over the page...

Method

Boil the potatoes until soft. Drain, peel and cut the potatoes into 2 cm (¾ in) cubes.

Heat the oil in a large non-stick frying pan on a medium heat. Add the mustard seeds, when they start to pop add the urad dhal and channa dhal stirring until slightly brown. Add the onions and cook until soft and translucent. Then add the ginger, chillies, curry leaves, turmeric, salt and asafoetida, stir well. Add the boiled potatoes, stir through until completely coated with spices. Add 240 ml (8 fl oz) of water and stir.

When the water starts to bubble lower the heat and cover the pan with a lid. Simmer for 10 minutes, until potatoes are soft and a lovely yellow color. Stir occasionally to prevent the potatoes from sticking to the pan and add more water if it gets dry, ideally you want the potatoes in a nice gravy.

Check for salt and adjust according to your taste. Finally add cilantro leaves, stir through and remove from the heat.

Aloo Mattar

(Green Peas and Potato)

Serves: 4 as part of a shared meal
Cooking Difficulty: Easy

A simple way to cook green peas and potatoes, cooked in flavors native to the north. To make a full meal of it prepare a simple Dhal (page 98) or Rajma (page 96) and eat with rice or Indian breads.

Ingredients

3 tablespoons ghee or canola oil
1 medium onion, finely diced
1 clove garlic, finely diced
2.5 cm (1 in) piece ginger, finely diced
1 teaspoon cumin seeds
2 teaspoons cilantro (coriander) powder
¼ teaspoon turmeric powder
½ teaspoon chilli powder
1 large tomato, roughly chopped
240 ml (8 fl oz) water
½ teaspoon salt
4 medium potatoes, peeled and cut into 2.5 cm (1 in) cubes
60 g (2 oz) peas, fresh or frozen
4 tablespoons cilantro (coriander), leaves and stems roughly chopped

Method

Heat the ghee in a deep frying pan on medium-high heat. Add the onion, garlic and ginger, and stir until the onion turns slightly brown. Add all the spices, stirring for a minute so that the spices release their aroma and form a paste.

Add the chopped tomatoes, 240 ml (8 fl oz) water and salt, stir well. Now add the potatoes and peas, stir and cook for 2 minutes. Cover with a lid, turn the heat down and simmer for 10 minutes, until the potatoes are cooked. Stir occasionally to prevent the potatoes from sticking to the pan and add more water if it dries out, ideally you want the potatoes in a nice gravy. The potatoes should be moist and well flavored by the onion and tomato paste.

Remove from the heat and transfer to a serving bowl and garnish with cilantro leaves.

Baingan Bharta
(Baked Eggplant in Spices)

Serves: 4 as part of a shared meal
Cooking Difficulty: Medium

Soft and smoky eggplant is blended with a base of tomatoes and spices to make a really lovely dish. The eggplant is baked in the oven, but if you want an added smoky flavor, once it's mostly cooked remove from the oven and, if you have a gas stove, char on an open flame until the skin is blistered and black.

This dish tastes particularly nice eaten with Lemon Rice (page 192), or Chapatis (page 178) and Raita (page 240).

Ingredients
1 large eggplant (aubergine)
3 tablespoons canola oil
1 medium red onion, finely diced
2 cm (¾ in) cube ginger, peeled and finely grated
1 clove garlic, finely grated
1 small hot green chilli, finely chopped
1 teaspoon garam masala **(page 284)**
1 teaspoon cumin powder
½ teaspoon cilantro (coriander) powder
½ teaspoon chilli powder (adjust to taste)
¼ teaspoon turmeric powder
½ teaspoon salt
4 medium ripe red tomatoes, roughly diced
Handful of cilantro (coriander), stalks and leaves roughly chopped

continued over the page…

Method

Place eggplant onto a tray and bake in a 180°C (350°F) oven. Bake the eggplant for 30 to 40 minutes until completely soft, turn the eggplant half way through so it cooks evenly. Once cooked, remove from the oven and allow to cool.

While the eggplant is cooking prepare your tomato base. Heat the oil in a large frying pan over a medium heat. Add the onion, ginger, garlic and green chilli. Stir for about 2 minutes until fragrant and the onions are soft and translucent.

Add all the spices and salt, stirring well to combine and cook for a minute. Add the diced tomatoes and 60 ml (2 fl oz) of water, stir well. Lower the heat, cover the pan with a lid and simmer gently for 10 minutes, stirring occasionally. Mash the tomatoes a little with a fork to make a chunky paste. Take the pan off the heat.

Once the eggplant is cool to touch, cut off it's top and then from the top peel the skin off using your fingers or a knife. Chop the peeled eggplant into long strips and then roughly dice it.

Place the pan with the tomato base back on a low heat, add the chopped eggplant. Using a fork, mash eggplant and tomato well, cook for a further 2 minutes for everything to infuse.

Garnish with cilantro leaves.

Cauliflower Fry

Serves: 4–6 as part of shared meal
Cooking Difficulty: Easy

After cooking cauliflower in this way you won't be able to look at it the same way. My brother actually prides himself on making this better than his wife, surprisingly most of us agree with him. The key is to cook the cauliflower really well so it's completely soft and gets a bit brown and crispy on the outside.

If you have any left over try it on toast for a savory breakfast or snack. Or when making a meal of it eat it with Rasam (page 105) or Sambar (page 131) and rice.

Ingredients
4 tablespoons canola oil
1 whole cauliflower, cut into small florets
2 teaspoons sambar powder (page 285), adjust to desired spice level)
¼ teaspoon turmeric powder
¼ teaspoon salt

Method
Heat oil in a large frying pan on medium-high heat. Add the cauliflower and spices, stir well until the cauliflower is yellow and well coated in the spice. Lower the heat, cover with a lid and allow the cauliflower to cook for 7 minutes.

Remove lid, stir the cauliflower, and continue to cook on a medium heat for 10 to 15 minutes, until cauliflower is completely soft and a bit crispy on the outside, remembering to stir occasionally to ensure the cauliflower cooks evenly.

Kathirikkai Fry

(Spicy Fried Eggplant)

Serves: 4 as part of a shared meal
Cooking Difficulty: Easy

A simple but tasty way to cook eggplant. It goes well with South Indian curries like Rasam (page 105) and Sambar (page 131), or Lemon (page 192) and Coconut (page 190) Rice.

Ingredients
4 tablespoons canola oil
1 medium red onion, sliced
1 teaspoon sambar powder **(page 285),** adjust to desired spice level)
½ teaspoon salt
¼ teaspoon turmeric
15 leaves curry leaves
1 large eggplant (aubergine), sliced into 3 x 4 cm (1 x 1.5 in) rectangles
1 tablespoon cilantro (coriander), stalks and leaves roughly chopped

Method
Heat 2 tablespoons of the oil in a frying pan over a medium heat. When hot, add the sliced onion and cook until soft and translucent. Lower the heat slightly then add all the spices, salt and curry leaves. Sprinkle with a bit of water to form a paste.

Add the sliced eggplant, stir well with the spices. Add the rest of the oil and stir well. Cover with a lid for 10 minutes, stirring occasionally. When the eggplant is tender but still firm, remove the lid and cook for another 2 minutes until the eggplant is completely soft.

Sprinkle with cilantro leaves.

Potato and Snake Beans

Serves: 4 as part of a shared meal
Cooking Difficulty: Easy

This dish is similar to Bindi Masala (page 142), and a nice way to try snake beans if you haven't eaten them before. They're usually in the asian section of a good green grocer, they're quite long and a bit more wrinkly in texture compared to a regular green bean. If you can't get your hands on them you can use green beans, they just won't crisp up in the same way. Eat with Chapatis (page 178) and yogurt for lunch.

Ingredients
4 tablespoons canola oil
1 medium red onion, finely sliced
1 teaspoon garam masala **(page 284)**
½ teaspoon chilli powder
¼ teaspoon turmeric
½ teaspoon salt
3 medium potatoes, peeled and cut into 2.5 cm (1 in) x 1 cm (½ in) pieces
1 small bunch snake beans, cut into 4 cm (1½ in) pieces
1 tablespoon cilantro (coriander), stalks and leaves roughly chopped

Method
Heat 2 tablespoons of oil in a frying pan over a medium heat. When hot, add the sliced onion and cook until soft and translucent. Lower the heat slightly then add the garam masala, chilli, turmeric and salt, stir well for a minute.

Add the potatoes and beans, stir well with the spice, then add the rest of the oil and stir well. Cover with a lid and cook for 10 to 15 minutes, stirring occasionally until the potatoes are completely cooked. Remove the lid and cook for another 2 minutes or so until the moisture evaporates and they're slightly crispy. Finish with cilantro leaves.

Eggplant and Zucchini Masala

Serves: 4–6 as part of a shared meal
Cooking Difficulty: Easy

I invented this dish when I had an abundance of summer zuchinni and eggplant. You could also add bell peppers (capsicum) and mushrooms to this mix. Serve with Chapatis (page 178) or you favorite Pulao.

Ingredients
2 tablespoons canola oil
1 medium red onion, finely chopped
10 curry leaves
1½ teaspoons sambar powder (page 285)
1 teaspoon cumin powder
¼ teaspoon turmeric
Pinch of asafoetida
1 teaspoon salt
4 medium tomatoes, diced
120 ml (4 fl oz) water
1 medium zucchini (courgette), cut into 2.5 cm (1 in) cubes
2 medium eggplants (aubergine), cut into 2.5 cm (1 in) cubes
Handful cilantro (coriander) leaves

Method
Heat the oil in a large non-stick frying pan over a medium heat. Add onion and cook until soft and translucent. Add the curry leaves, all the spices and salt, stir well to combine. Then add the diced tomatoes and 120 ml (4 fl oz) of water, stir. Lower the heat and cover with a lid to simmer for 5 minutes. By now the tomatoes should be completely soft, remove the lid and using a potato masher crush the mixture to make a chunky paste.

Next, add the zucchini and eggplant and mix well with the tomatoes. Cover with a lid and cook for 10 minutes on a medium heat, stirring occasionally. Once the vegetables are soft, add cilantro leaves and transfer to a serving bowl.

Aloo Masala

(North Indian Style Potatoes)

Serves: 4–6 as part of a shared meal
Cooking Difficulty: Easy

The yogurt and garam masala make this a North indian version of Masala Potato (page 147). Just like it's South Indian counterpart it's a gravy style dish, this one is best eaten with Biryani (page 211), Parathas (page 170) or your favorite Pulao.

Ingredients
2 large potatoes
1 tablespoon canola oil
¼ teaspoon cumin seeds
1 red onion, roughly chopped
½ teaspoon garam masala (page 284)
½ teaspoon chilli powder (adjust to taste)
¼ teaspoon turmeric powder
½ teaspoon salt
1 tablespoon natural yogurt
1 large tomato, roughly chopped
120 ml (4 fl oz) water
Handful cilantro (coriander) leaves

Method

Boil the potatoes until tender. Drain and allow to cool slightly before peeling and cutting them into 3 cm (1¼ in) chunks.

Heat the oil in a large non-stick frying pan over a medium heat. Add the cumin seeds and stir for a few seconds, then add the onions and cook until soft and translucent. Add all the spices and salt, stir for few seconds. Now add the yogurt and stir to form a paste. Add the chopped tomatoes and stir for another minute, then add 60 ml (2 fl oz) of the water and lower the heat to simmer the mixture for 2 minutes.

Once the tomatoes are soft, mash them with a potato masher to make a thick gravy. Add the cooked potatoes and the rest of the water, stir well. Cover the pan and simmer for 5 minutes until the potatoes are tender and have absorbed the spice. If too dry add a bit more water to make a thick gravy.

To finish tear up the cilantro leaves and sprinkle over the potatoes.

Cabbage Thoran
(Dry Fried Cabbage with Coconut)

Serves: 4
Cooking Difficulty: Easy

This is a no fuss way to cook up some vegetables to accompany any South Indian meal. Thoran is a technique of lightly cooking vegetables with coconut, mustard seeds, urad dhal and curry leaves giving it a light but vibrant flavor. You can use several other vegetables like beans, carrots and spinach, my daughter has even made a kale thoran. Below is the traditional Tamil recipe, but in Kerela they also add turmeric and cumin seeds for color and flavor, try it both ways and see what you prefer.

Every time my daughter returns home she always requests I make Rasam (page 105), Rice and Cabbage Thoran.

Ingredients
2 teaspoons canola oil
½ teaspoon black mustard seeds
3 whole dried red chillies, roughly torn
1 teaspoon urad dhal
Sprinkle asafoetida
¼ head of cabbage, really finely sliced into long strips
15 curry leaves
1 teaspoon salt
2 tablespoons desiccated or grated fresh coconut **(page 280)**
Handful cilantro (coriander), leaves and stems roughly chopped

Method
Heat the oil in a frying pan on a medium heat. Add the mustard seeds and when they start to pop, add the urad dhal, dried chillies and asafoetida. Stir until urad dhal turns slightly brown. Then quickly add the cabbage, curry leaves and salt, stir well. Lower the heat then cover the pan and let the cabbage cook for a few minutes until it is completely cooked, stirring occasionally. Add coconut, stir through and cook for another minute.

Sprinkle with cilantro leaves and transfer to a serving bowl.

Spicy Potato Fry

Serves: 4
Cooking Difficulty: Easy

Be warned once you make these spicy potatoes you'll find it hard to resist making them over and over again. It's a really common way that we cook potatoes in our house, and they go perfectly on the side of Rasam (page 105) and Sambar (page 131) with rice or just with Coconut (page 190) or Lemon (page 192) Rice.

I used to send my daughter off with leftover potatoes stuffed in a sandwich for lunch, it soon became one of her favorite lunches.

Ingredients
4 large potatoes
4 tablespoons canola oil
1 teaspoon black mustard seeds
1 teaspoon urad dhal
Sprinkle asafoetida
½ teaspoon turmeric powder
1 tablespoon sambar powder **(page 285)**
15 curry leaves, picked and roughly torn
½ teaspoon salt

Method
Wash the potatoes and cut them into small 1 cm (½ in) cubes.

Heat the oil in a large non-stick frying pan on a medium heat. Add the mustard seeds, when they start to pop immediately add urad dhal and asafoetida, stirring until slightly brown. Now add turmeric and sambar powder, stir well. Add the cubed potatoes, curry leaves and salt, stir well. Turn the heat down slightly, cover the pan and cook for 10 minutes, stirring occasionally.

Remove the lid and cook the potatoes for another few minutes until completely cooked and slightly crunchy on the outside.

Breads

Paratha

(Flaky Flat Bread)

Makes 8–10
Cooking Difficulty: Medium

Parathas are a beautiful flaky Indian flatbread, most commonly found in households of North India. They can be eaten simply for breakfast with lemon and pickle, or even plain with a hot cup of masala tea. We didn't eat them often growing up as they fell into my Dad's category of an occasional treat. When they did feature on our family's menu, they were served with a hearty vegetable kurma and mint raita.

This recipe for parathas will get you beautiful fresh flat breads in just over half an hour. There are also a few stuffed varieties, potato (page 173) and raddish (page 176), to try after you've learnt how to make this basic one.

Ingredients
375 g (13.2 oz) atta flour*, plus extra for dusting
¾ teaspoon salt
2 tablespoons canola oil
300 ml (10 fl oz) water
6 tablespoons ghee

* If you can't get atta you can also use half wholemeal and half plain flour as a substitute

Method

Step one
In a mixing bowl, mix the flour and salt. Make a well in the middle and add oil, then gradually add water and mix to form a dough, the dough shouldn't be too sticky. If it is too sticky add a bit more flour, if dough is too dry sprinkle with more water. Form a rough ball incorporating all the flour in the bowl. Tip out onto a lightly floured surface, knead for a few minutes until you have a firm and smooth dough. Place the ball back into the mixing bowl, cover with a moist kitchen towel or plastic wrap. Leave to rest for 20 minutes.

Step two
Place a bit of atta flour and the ghee into separate small bowls and keep to the side. Lightly dust flour on a clean kitchen surface or wooden board for rolling.

Divide the dough into balls about the size of a lime, you should get 8 to 10 balls. To roll the parathas, take a ball, lightly coat in flour and roll into a 10 cm (4 in) circle about 2–3 mm (⅛ in) thick. Spread ¼ teaspoon of ghee evenly on top of the circle, then fold in half to make a semi-circle. Spread a little bit more ghee evenly on top, and then fold again to make a triangle. Press the open edge of the triangle to lightly seal. Lightly dust in flour then roll out to a larger triangle, until it's about 3 mm (⅛ in) thick. As you're rolling out you'll need to flip the triangle over and lightly flour with extra atta flour. Place to the side, cover with a moist tea towel. Repeat with the rest of the dough.

Step three
Heat a heavy-based frying pan on a high heat. Once the pan is hot, place one of the parathas down, when dough starts to pull and lift slightly, drizzle ghee around edges and lightly brush some on top. Once the bottom is slightly brown, use a spatula to flip over, brush with a bit more ghee and allow the other side to cook. Cook until both sides have lovely brown patches all over. Remove from the pan and place on a plate with a paper towel, spread a final bit of ghee on top. Cook the rest in the same way.

Aloo Paratha
(Flat Bread Stuffed with Potato)

Serves: 10–12
Cooking Difficulty: Hard

In 1984 I got married and even though I never had a desire to travel the world, I ended up in Darwin Australia. The tropical weather and coconuts were familiar, but that's where it stopped. There were no spice shops or Indian restaurants, so connecting with the small Indian community was a way to stay close to home.

It was here that we made some Punjabi friends and we would often go over to their place for lunch, where we were served a simple meal of stuffed paratha, pickle, yogurt and maybe a simple vegetable dish like Bindi Masala (page 142).

It was nice to still be learning new things about my own country even when we were so far away from home. As usual after eating something new I peppered the host with questions getting all the details of the dish, then practiced and perfected the dish myself at home. My version of this dish has a bit more spice than what I was served, my Dad would have loved it.

Ingredients
For the dough
1 portion Paratha (page 170)

For the filling
2 medium potatoes, boiled and mashed
¼ teaspoon garam masala (page 284)
¼ teaspoon cumin powder
¼ teaspoon salt
1 green chilli, finely chopped (optional)
2 tablespoons cilantro (coriander), leaves very finely chopped

continued over the page...

Method

Step one
First make your dough, as per step one of the paratha recipe **on page 170**.

Step two
Mash the potatoes until soft and smooth. Add garam masala, cumin powder, chillies, cilantro leaves and salt. Mix well ensuring spices are well blended with the potatoes. Cool completely.

Step three
Once the filling has cooled and the dough has rested for 20 minutes you can make the parathas.

Place a bit of atta flour and the ghee into separate small bowls and keep to the side. Lightly dust flour on a clean kitchen surface or wooden board for rolling.

Divide the dough into balls about the size of a lime, you should get 8 to 10 balls. Lightly coat a ball in flour and roll out to a 10 cm (4 in) circle. Take 1 tablespoon of potato mix, place in the middle of a rolled dough, pull the edges up to form a ball, making sure there are no gaps or holes. Gently press the ball down to make a flat disc, lightly dust with flour and gently roll out to a larger circle about 3 mm (⅛ in) thick, it should be around a 15 cm (6 in) circle. It takes time to master the right thickness and shape, just keep experimenting and learn what works. When rolling if there are any tears, use plain dough to patch up, dust with a bit of flour and continue to gently roll out. Set aside under a moist towel and repeat with remaining filling and dough.

Step four
Cook as per step three of the paratha recipe **on page 170**.

Muli Paratha

(Flat Bread Stuffed with Radish)

Makes: 8–10
Cooking Difficulty: Hard

These stand alone as a really tasty snack. The raddish just tastes wonderful tucked into the paratha and they're great to take on a picnic just don't forget the chilli pickle.

Ingredients
For the dough
1 portion paratha **(page 170)**

For the filling
1 teaspoon canola oil
300 g (10.5 oz) coarsely grated radish
½ teaspoon garam masala **(page 284)**
¼ teaspoon cumin powder
1 green chilli, finely chopped
¼ teaspoon salt
2 tablespoons cilantro (coriander), leaves very finely chopped

Method

Step one
First make your dough, as per step one of the paratha recipe on **page 170**.

Step two
While the dough is resting prepare the radish filling. Heat the oil in a frying pan on medium-high heat. Add the grated radish, garam masala, cumin powder, chillies and salt. Cook for 2 minutes until radish is soft. Remove from heat, stir through cilantro. Cool.

Step three
Once the filling has cooled and the dough has rested for 20 minutes you can make the parathas.

Place a bit of atta flour and the ghee into separate small bowls and keep to the side. Lightly dust flour on a clean kitchen surface or wooden board for rolling.

Divide the dough into balls about the size of a lime, you should get 8 to 10 balls. Lightly coat a ball in flour and roll out to a 10 cm (4 in) circle. Take 1 tablespoon of radish mix, place in the middle of the rolled dough, pull the edges up to form a ball, making sure there are no gaps or holes. Gently press the ball down to make a flat disc, lightly dust with flour and gently roll out to a larger circle about 3 mm (⅛ in) thick, it should be about a 15 cm (6 in) circle. It takes time to master the right thickness and shape, just keep experimenting and learn what works. When rolling if there are any tears, use plain dough to patch up, dust with a bit of flour and continue to gently roll out. Set aside under a moist towel and repeat with remaining filling and dough.

Step four
Cook as per step three of the paratha recipe **on page 170.**

Chapati
(Puffed Flat Bread)

Makes: 10–12
Cooking Difficulty: Hard

Chapatis are a simple bread found in homes all over India, the light and simple bread is eaten at lunch or for a light dinner with a simple dhal and vegetables like Bindi Masala (page 142), Aloo Masala (page 162) or Baingan Bharta (page 152).

When it comes to making chapatis they're simple but it can also take time to get the knack of making the right shape and also the right thickness for it to puff. You might need to experiment in your rolling before you get it right, but don't despair even if they don't puff they're still tasty.

Ingredients
300 g (10.5 oz) atta flour, plus extra 30 g (1 oz) for dusting
¼ teaspoon salt
180–240 ml (6–8 fl oz) warm water
4 tablespoons ghee

Method
In a mixing bowl, mix flour and salt together. Make a well in the middle and gradually add just enough warm water (anywhere in between 180–240 ml/6 fl oz–8 fl oz) until you can bring the dough together and it's a bit crumbly, not sticky. Using your hands bring the dough together to form a ball, if too dry add a bit more warm water. Once a ball forms, tip out onto a floured surface and keep kneading until the dough is soft but not sticky when you pinch it. You should be able to roll a ball until it's completely smooth with no cracks, add tiny bits of warm water or flour as needed. Divide the dough into balls about the size of a small lime. Place back into the clean mixing bowl, cover with a damp tea towel and set aside for 30 minutes.

continued over the page...

Lightly flour a ball, and roll out to a circle of about 13 to 15 cm (6 in) and 3 mm (⅛ in) thick. Spread a bit of atta flour on the rolled chapati, set aside and cover with a damp tea towel to prevent from drying out.

Heat a heavy-based frying pan on a medium-high heat, it should be nice and hot before you cook the chapati. Place a chapati down in the hot frying pan, when bubbles appear all over and it slightly puffs flip to the other side. As the chapati continues to puff gently press with a folded tea towel to encourage the chapati to puff up. (If it doesn't puff up that's okay, it will still taste good, it takes time to learn how to roll for the right thickness just keep experimenting and see what works.) Once there are dark brown bubbles on the both sides, use tongs to remove it from the pan. Transfer to a plate, cover with a ¼ teaspoon of ghee and cover with a tea towel to prevent it drying out. Repeat for remaining dough.

Puri

(Deep-Fried Puffed Breads)

Makes: 12–15 puris, enough to serve 4 people as part of a full meal
Cooking Difficulty: Medium

Puris make the perfect brunch or lunch, breads that magically puff up when deep fried. Eat them straight away and gently tear off a piece and eat with Masala Potato (page 147) or Cauliflower Kurma (page 88) and Mixed Raita (page 241). My kids used to have puri eating competitions, I think my son won with 12. For non-competition eaters, 2 or 3 with sides is usually enough for a serve.

Ingredients
190 g (6.7 oz) wholemeal flour
¼ teaspoon salt
120 ml–180 ml (4–6 fl oz) water
60 ml (2 fl oz) canola oil, for rolling
Canola oil for deep frying

Method
In a mixing bowl, mix the flour and salt together. Make a small well and pour in 120 ml (4 fl oz) of water, using your hands gently mix with the flour, it should be crumbly, not sticky. Bring mix together to form a ball, tip out onto a lightly dusted surface, knead until a firm dough forms, add extra water as needed. Divide the dough to make small balls about half the size of a lime. You should get 12 to 15. You can start to make puris straight away. If preparing the dough in advance place in an airtight container in the fridge and bring back to room temperature before using.

continued over the page...

Dip the ball into a little bit of oil, then use a rolling pin, roll out each ball into 10 cm (4 in) circles about 3 mm (⅛ in) thick. If the dough sticks to the rolling pin, use a little bit more oil on the dough. Set aside and cover with a towel. Repeat for remaining dough.

Fill a deep frying pan two thirds full with canola oil, heat on a medium-high heat. Heat oil until very hot, and almost slightly smoky. Slide one puri in the oil at a time. The bread should start to bubble, if it doesn't wait a bit longer for the oil to get hot, if it bubbles too quickly and burns the puri take off the heat and allow to cool. Use the back of a slotted spoon to gently push the puri down into the oil, encouraging it to puff up. A few seconds after it's puffed, gently flip the puri over and cook the other side until golden brown. Lift the puri out of the oil, and drain on a paper towel. Cook the rest and serve immediately with your chosen side dishes.

Rice

Brinji Rice
(Creamy Coconut Rice)

Serves: 6–8 as part of a shared meal
Cooking Difficulty: Easy

When I was growing up I used to spend hours at my friends place after school. They had a chef who prepared all the meals and always had something waiting for us when we got home. It was there that I tried Brinji Rice for the first time, I absolutely loved the rich creaminess of the coconut and aromatic spices. My curiosity sparked a chat with the chef who generously shared his recipe with me.

I went home excitedly that night to share my new discovery with my Mum, who made a few tweaks to recreate her own version of the dish. She added cashews for texture and tomatoes and chilli to balance the creaminess of the coconut. We ate it with Masala Potato (page 147) and Mixed Raita (page 241). Fry some pappadums to give the meal a bit of crunch.

Ingredients
310 g (10.6 oz) basmati rice
5 tablespoons ghee or canola oil
70 g (2.5 oz) whole cashews
2–3 bay leaves
2 whole star anise
4 whole green cardamom
1 cinnamon stick
2 red onions, thinly sliced
4–6 small hot green chillies, sliced into half lengthwise
5 cm (2 in) piece ginger, finely grated
3 cloves garlic, finely grated
1 medium tomato, finely diced
1 green bell pepper (capsicum), cut into long thin strips
¼ teaspoon turmeric powder
350 ml (12 fl oz) light coconut milk
350 ml (12 fl oz) water
1 teaspoon salt

Method

Wash the rice until the water runs clear, drain and set aside.

Heat ghee or oil in a deep frying pan on medium-high heat for a minute. Add cashews, bay leaves, star anise, cardamom and cinnamon and stir for 30 seconds. Add the onions and cook until golden. Then add the chillies, ginger and garlic, stir for a further 30 seconds. Add tomatoes, bell pepper and turmeric, stir for a few minutes until the tomatoes soften and reduce. Add the washed rice and stir for another minute. Finally add the coconut milk, water and salt. Bring to the boil, reduce the heat, cover with a lid and simmer for 15 minutes until the rice is cooked and fluffy.

Gently spoon the rice out on to a serving platter, allowing the rice to steam.

Thenga Sadam
(Coconut Rice)

Serves: 6–8 as part of a meal
Cooking Difficulty: Easy

Religious festivals in India are lively affairs, smoky fires, chanting of prayers, ringing of bells, and the preparation of a special meal. For the south Indian full moon festival and Tamil New Year, we prepare a meal with three kinds of rice – Lemon (page 192), Coconut and Tamarind.

This rice is also eaten widely outside of festival times, taken on picnics as it tastes just as good cold, and goes perfectly with a side of Potato Fry (page 166) or Spicy Fried Eggplant (page 157). For something slightly different, try substituting rice for steamed vermicelli.

Ingredients
2 tablespoons canola oil
1 teaspoon black mustard seeds
2 tablespoon cashew nuts, roughly chopped
1½ teaspoon urad dhal
2 teaspoons channa dhal or yellow split peas
2 dried red chillies, torn in half
75 g (3 oz) desiccated or fresh grated coconut (page 280)
½ teaspoon salt
15 curry leaves, roughly torn
400 g (14 oz) basmati rice, cooked (page 279)
2 tablespoons cilantro (coriander) leaves, finely chopped

Method:
Heat oil in a deep frying pan on a medium-high heat for a minute. Add the mustard seeds when they start to pop, immediately add the cashew nuts, urad and channa dhal, stirring until slightly brown. Add the chillies, coconut, salt and curry leaves, stir for 30 seconds.

Gently fold through rice and salt until well combined. Turn off heat and finally stir through cilantro leaves.

Elumichai Sadam

(Lemon Rice)

Serves: 6–8 as part of a shared meal
Cooking Difficulty: Easy

This is a common rice dish eaten in Tamil Nadu. It's often featured on special occasions, but most often it's wrapped in a banana leaf and packed up for long train trips and picnics.

Bring it along for your next picnic, adding some toasted almonds to make it a bit more substantial. It looks perfect on a plate served with Potato Fry (page 166), any eggplant dish, and Carrot Salad (page 234) for color and texture.

Ingredients
2 tablespoons canola oil
1 teaspoon black mustard seeds
30 g (1 oz) cashew nuts, roughly chopped
2 teaspoons urad dhal
2 teaspoons channa dhal or yellow split peas
2 small hot green chillies, finely chopped
5 cm (2 in) piece ginger, finely grated
¼ teaspoon turmeric powder
15 curry leaves, roughly torn
2 lemons, juiced
1 teaspoon salt
400 g (14 oz) basmati rice, cooked (page 279)
2 tablespoons cilantro (coriander), leaves and stalks chopped

Method:
Heat oil in a deep frying pan on medium heat. Add mustard seeds, when they start to pop immediately add cashew nuts, urad dhal and channa dhal, stirring until slightly brown.

Reduce the heat, then add chillies, ginger, turmeric powder and curry leaves. Stir quickly for 10 seconds. Turn off the heat, and add lemon juice and salt, stir to combine well.

Now add the cooked rice and gently stir through until completely coated and yellow. Taste and adjust salt and lemon to taste. Stir through the cilantro. Transfer to a serving dish.

Thakali Sadam

(Tomato Rice)

Serves: 6–8 as part of a shared meal.
Cooking Difficulty: Easy

A great way to use ripe tomatoes in summer. My mum used to make this for me to take for lunch, along with Cauliflower Fry (page 156) or Potato Fry (page 166), crunchy pappadums and Mixed Raita (page 241). It also makes a great picnic food.

Ingredients
4 tablespoons canola oil
2 bay leaves
1 red onion, finely diced
5 cm (2 in) piece ginger, finely grated
1 clove garlic, finely grated
1 teaspoon garam masala (page 284)
½ teaspoon cumin powder
½ teaspoon chilli powder
¼ teaspoon turmeric powder
2 medium ripe tomatoes, finely chopped
½ teaspoon salt
400 g (14 oz) basmati rice, cooked (page 279)
2 tablespoons mint leaves, chopped

Method
Heat the oil in a deep frying pan on medium-high heat. Add the bay leaves and onion, cook until the onion is soft and translucent. Add the ginger and garlic, stir for 30 seconds. Then add all the dry spices, stir until well blended.

Add the tomatoes and salt, cook for 2 minutes until tomatoes start to soften and release their juice. Lower the heat, cover the pan and simmer for 2 to 3 minutes until the tomato mixture reduces to a thick paste. Turn off the heat.

Add the cooked basmati rice and chopped mint leaves, fold through until the rice is completely coated with the rich tomato paste.

Thayir Sadam

(Yogurt Rice)

Serves: 4 as part of a full meal
Cooking Difficulty: Easy

When I get together with my Indian friends we often have a potluck lunch, to share the load of cooking. I always get asked to bring this yogurt rice. You need mushy rice for this dish, cooking the rice with more water than usual and cooling with ice cubes usually does the trick. Buttermilk gives the dish a smoother texture, but if it's not on hand you can leave it out.

Yogurt aids digestion, so it's traditionally eaten at the end of a meal. The dish can also stand alone, eaten with a bit of pickle, Sambar (page 131) and Vegetable Fry.

Ingredients
200 g (7 oz) long grain rice
700 ml (1½ pints) water
475 ml (1 pint) natural yogurt
120 ml (4 fl oz) buttermilk
1 teaspoon salt
1 tablespoon canola oil
1 teaspoon black mustard seeds
1½ teaspoon urad dhal
1 ½ teaspoon channa dhal or yellow split pea
2 small hot green chillies, finely chopped
2.5 cm (1 in) piece ginger, grated
¼ teaspoon asafoetida
20 curry leaves, roughly torn
2 tablespoons cilantro (coriander), stalks and leaves finely chopped

continued over the page...

Method

Wash the rice until the water runs clear and drain. Place the rice with water in a saucepan over a high heat, bring to the boil, stirring occasionally to ensure the rice doesn't stick to the bottom of the pan. Once boiling turn the heat down low, stir once more then cover with a lid and let the rice cook for 10 minutes. When the rice is completely soft, transfer to a large bowl, and stir through 15 ice cubes. Cool for 15 minutes.

Whisk the yogurt, buttermilk and salt in a bowl until smooth, set aside.

Heat the oil in a small heavy-based frying pan on a medium heat, add the mustard seeds, when they pop, add urad and channa dhal, stirring until slightly brown. Then add the chillies, ginger, asafoetida and curry leaves, it will sputter a little, stir for 10 seconds. Turn off the heat and pour over the yogurt. Add cilantro leaves, stir well and refrigerate.

Once the rice is cool, use a potato masher to mash up a bit. Pour the yogurt mixture over the rice, and mix well. Taste for salt and adjust according to taste.

Transfer to a serving dish.

Bisi Bele Bath

(South Indian Spicy Risotto)

Serves: 4
Cooking difficulty: Medium

This is a typical dish from Karanataka in the southern part of India and a recipe that my Mum learnt when visiting relatives in Bangalore, the states capital. We all loved it so she made it at home quite frequently, plus she loved it because it was wholesome and such an easy meal to prepare. It comes out looking quite mushy, but trust me it tastes *much* better than it looks.

Eat with Mixed Raita (page 241) and crunchy potato chips or fried pappadums on the side.

Ingredients
Spice mix
2 tablespoons cilantro (coriander) seeds
6-8 dried red chillies (adjust according to taste)
1 tablespoon channa dhal or yellow split peas
4 cm (1½ in) piece cinnamon stick
6 whole cloves
40 g (1.5 oz) desiccated or fresh grated coconut (page 280)

1 tablespoon firmly packed dried tamarind or 1 teaspoon tamarind paste
200 g (7 oz) long grain rice
130 g (4 oz) toor dhal or red lentils
1½ teaspoon salt
½ teaspoon turmeric powder
1.4 litres (3 pints) water
5 tablespoons ghee
1 carrot, cut into 1 cm (½ in) cubes
15 green beans, cut into 1 cm (½ in) pieces
¼ head cauliflower, cut into chunky florets
40 g (1.5 oz) green peas, fresh or frozen
1 red onion, finely sliced
6 tablespoons cilantro (coriander), leaves roughly chopped

Method

To make your spice mix, heat 1 teaspoon of ghee in a small frying pan add all the ingredients and roast until the channa dhal and coconut are slightly brown. Remove from heat and cool. Once cooled, place into a spice grinder and process to a coarse powder, set aside.

Soak the dried tamarind in 120 ml (4 fl oz) of warm water for 10 minutes. Squeeze the softened tamarind with your hand and mix it well in the water, strain through a sieve and set aside. If you're using tamarind paste simply stir it with 120 ml (4 fl oz) warm water and set aside.

Wash rice and lentils together, drain and set aside.

Place rice, lentils, 950 ml (2 pints) of water, ¼ teaspoon turmeric and ½ teaspoon salt in a large saucepan, and cook on a medium-high heat. Bring to the boil, stir well then lower the heat, cover with a lid and simmer for 15 minutes, until rice is almost cooked.

Heat 1 tablespoon ghee in a deep frying pan over a medium-high heat. Add all the vegetables except the onion, stir well and cook for 2 minutes. Add the tamarind juice, ¼ teaspoon turmeric powder, 1 teaspoon salt and 475 ml (1 pint) of water. When the water starts to boil lower the heat and continue to cook until vegetables are almost cooked. Now add the ground spice mix and cook for 2 more minutes.

Pour the cooked vegetables into the saucepan with the cooked rice, stir until everything is well incorporated and cook on a low heat for 5 minutes to get a thick risotto like consistency. Transfer to a serving dish.

Heat the remaining ghee in a small frying pan on a medium heat, add the onion and cook until caramelized and crispy brown. Garnish with the crispy onions and cilantro.

Indian Fried Rice

Serves: 6–8 as part of a full meal
Cooking difficulty: Easy

My eldest brother used to run a catering business from the roof of the apartment block. Despite the humble setup, thatched roofs built from palm trees and simple gas hobs, the chefs used to produce all kinds of wonders that were packaged up and sent across Chennai.

This simple rice dish was made to complement the curry special of the day, it doesn't use any spices, and instead gets its delicate flavor from onion, garlic and ginger cooked in ghee. It's perfect to eat with Paneer Matar (page 103), Paneer Kofta Curry (page 110) or Sodhi (page 86).

Ingredients
400 g (14 oz) basmati rice
1 green bell pepper (capsicum)
¼ head cabbage
1 carrot
10 green beans
885 ml (29 fl oz) water
3 tablespoons ghee or canola oil
1 red onion, finely sliced
1 small hot green chilli (optional)
2 cloves garlic, finely grated
5 cm (2 in) piece ginger, finely grated
1 teaspoon salt

Method

Wash the rice thoroughly until the water runs clear (this removes the starch which makes fluffier rice). Cover the rice with plenty of cold water and soak for 15 minutes, drain.

Remove the seeds from the bell pepper and then finely slice lengthways into long strips. Cut the cabbage and carrot in the same way. Cut the beans finely on an angle.

Bring the water to the boil in a large saucepan. Add the washed rice and boil for a minute, stirring to make sure the rice doesn't stick to the bottom of the pan. Lower the heat, cover with a lid and simmer gently for 15 minutes. The rice is cooked when the grains on top start to stand up. When that happens remove from the heat, and carefully tip the rice out onto a large platter fluffing up with a fork.

Heat the ghee in a large frying pan on a medium heat. Add the sliced onion, chillies (if using) garlic and ginger. When the onion turns slightly brown add all the vegetables and stir for a minute. Lower the heat and cook until vegetables are cooked but still have a little crunch. Gently fold through the cooked rice.

Jeera Pulao
(Cumin Flavored Rice)

Serves: 6–8 as part of a full meal
Cooking Difficulty: Easy

A simple rice dish flavored with ghee and cumin seeds. Perfect if you want something special to eat with your curry and vegetables.

One of the most comforting meals is to eat this rice with my Simple Dhal (page 98) and a dollop of Mixed Raita (page 241).

Ingredients
400 g (14 oz) basmati rice
2 tablespoons ghee or canola oil
1 teaspoon cumin seeds
1 litre (2 pints) of water
¼ teaspoon salt

Method
Wash the rice thoroughly until the water runs clear (this removes the starch which makes fluffier rice). Cover the rice with plenty of cold water and soak for 15 minutes, drain.

Heat ghee or oil in a large heavy based saucepan on a medium heat. Add cumin seeds, and allow them to slightly sizzle and release their aroma, being careful not to burn.

Tip the drained rice into the pan and stir to coat in ghee and cumin seeds. Add water and salt, stir well.

Bring to the boil, then lower the heat, cover with a lid and simmer for 15 minutes. You'll know the rice is cooked when the grains of rice start to stand upright. Never stir rice while cooking, once cooked gently tip it out onto a platter and use a fork to fluff up the rice, allow to steam.

Peas and Mint Pulao

Serves: 4 as part of a shared meal
Cooking Difficulty: Easy

Peas and mint, a tried and tested combination, come together beautifully to flavor this simple pulao. A special rice dish to serve alongside Vegetable Kurma (page 108) or any of my paneer dishes.

Ingredients
400 g (14 oz) basmati rice
3 tablespoons ghee or canola oil
1 medium red onion, finely sliced
1 small hot green chilli (optional)
150 g (5 oz) peas, fresh or frozen
40 g (1.5 oz) fresh mint leaves, roughly chopped
885 ml (29 fl oz) water
1 teaspoon salt

Method
Wash the rice thoroughly until the water runs clear (this removes the starch which makes fluffier rice). Cover the rice with plenty of cold water and soak for 15 minutes, drain.

Heat ghee or oil in a large frying pan on a medium heat. Add the sliced onion and chilli, cook until the onion starts to brown.

Add the peas and mint leaves, stir for a minute. Then add the drained rice, stir for 2 minutes. Add water and salt, stir well. Bring to the boil, give another stir then cover with a lid, lower the heat and cook for 15 minutes until the rice is cooked. You'll know the rice is cooked when the grains of rice start to stand upright. Once cooked gently tip it out onto a platter and use a fork to fluff up the rice, allow to steam.

Pongal
(Creamy Lentils and Rice)

Serves: 4 as part of a shared meal
Cooking Difficulty: Easy

Religious festivals in India often bring up many warm childhood memories of foods, songs and rituals. The festival of Pongal is particularly special, cooking over an open fire outside where you place a clay pot and cook a rice mixture until it bubbles over to "pongu," a Tamil word. It's a festival to give thanks to the sun, earth and animals for a healthy harvest and it's also a time to give thanks to the farmers on the land who work hard to provide us with food.

There's two kinds of pongal a sweet variety and a savory one. This recipe is for the savory one which has a creamy risotto like texture and is gently spiced with black pepper and cumin, and roasted cashews. It's a popular breakfast dish all year round, eat it with piping hot Sambar (page 131) and Coconut Chutney (page 242).

Ingredients
200 g (7 oz) basmati rice
110 g (3.8 oz) yellow moong dhal
8 tablespoons ghee
3 tablespoons cashew nuts, roughly chopped
1 teaspoon black peppercorns
1 teaspoon cumin seeds
1 ½ teaspoon finely chopped ginger
20 curry leaves
950 ml (2 pints) water
½ teaspoon salt

continued over the page...

Method

Place the rice and lentils in a large bowl, wash thoroughly until the water runs clear, drain and set aside.

Gently heat 5 tablespoons of ghee in a heavy based saucepan. Add 2 tablespoons of the cashew nuts, when they start to brown add the peppercorns and cumin seeds. Stir for a few seconds, then add the ginger and most of the curry leaves. Add the drained rice and lentils and stir for a minute, then add the water and salt, stir well to ensure the rice isn't stuck to the bottom or sides of the pan.

Bring to the boil and stir once more. Reduce to a simmer and cover pan with a tight lid. While cooking if the mixture bubbles up over the pot, keep the lid slightly ajar to let the steam out. Cook for 15 to 20 minutes until the rice and moong dhal are soft and mushy, the consistency should be like a risotto.

Once cooked, remove from the heat and gently spoon into a serving dish. To finish, heat the remaining 3 tablespoons of ghee in a small saucepan then add the remaining cashews and curry leaves. Once the cashews are golden, pour over the rice. Stir well.

Vegetable Biryani

Serves: 6 as part of a shared meal
Cooking Difficulty: Medium

Biryanis are better known in the north, where there are influences of Mogul kings and Iranian cuisine and culture are prominent but that didn't stop my Dad, a traditional South Indian Hindu, from learning and creating his own version of the dish.

We had a biryani day once a month, memories I keep closest to my heart. It brought everyone together, my Mum got the day off, and each of my brothers and sister were assigned roles: chopping vegetables, washing rice, as the youngest I got the best job, grinding spices. I used a stone slate and rolling pin to grind everything fresh, following my Dad's instructions on how to grind each spice just so and balancing the amounts to get the perfect combination for the biryani, later this is where I got the inspiration for my own recipe of garam masala (page 284).

When it was done, we would all sit together as a family, eating generous serves of Biryani with Vegetable (page 108) or Cauliflower Kurma (page 88) and Raita (page 240) on the side.

Ingredients
400 g (14 oz) basmati rice
8 tablespoons ghee or canola oil
6 cm (2½ in) cinnamon stick, broken into 2 pieces
4 green cardamom pods
1 red onion, finely diced
3 cloves garlic, finely grated
2 x 5 cm (2 in) ginger, finely grated
1 teaspoon garam masala
¼ teaspoon turmeric powder
¼ teaspoon chilli powder (adjust to taste)
1 small hot green chilli (adjust to taste)
60 ml (2 fl oz) natural yogurt
1 carrot, chopped into 2.5 cm (1 in) cubes

15 fresh green beans, chopped into 3 cm (1¼ in) pieces
1 medium potato, chopped into 2.5 cm (1 in) cubes
20 g (¾ oz) fresh mint leaves
700 ml (1½ pints) water

Method

Wash the rice thoroughly until the water runs clear (this removes the starch which makes fluffier rice). Cover the rice with plenty of cold water and soak for 15 minutes, drain.

Heat a large heavy-based frying pan and heat the ghee or oil. When hot, add cinnamon and cardamom, stir for a few seconds. Add the onion and cook until soft and translucent, then add the garlic and ginger, cook until the onion browns. Now add the rest of the spices and chilli, mix well. Add the yogurt and quickly stir for 30 seconds.

Now add the chopped vegetables, mint leaves and stir until everything is well combined. Add the washed basmati rice, stir well and cook for a few minutes. Now add water and salt, stirring to ensure rice isn't stuck to the bottom of the pan. When the water starts to bubble, lower the heat, give the mix another stir. Cover with the lid and simmer for 15 minutes until the rice is cooked, it should be plump and fluffy. Gently stir through to distribute vegetables and spices evenly, and transfer to a large serving dish.

Rava Kichidi

(Semolina with Vegetables)

Serves: 4–6
Cooking Difficulty: Easy

A light and nourishing dish, the semolina is roasted and cooked with just enough water to be soft and spongy. You can make a quicker version by omitting the whole spices and throwing in whatever vegetables you have on hand.

Serve with Coconut Chutney (page 242), pickle and yogurt.

Ingredients
250 g (8.8 oz) semolina
3 tablespoons ghee or canola oil
1 teaspoon black mustard seeds
1 stick cinnamon
2 bay leaves
4 cloves cardamom
1 red onion, finely diced
5 cm (2 in) piece ginger, finely chopped
2 small hot green chillies, cut lengthwise
15 curry leaves, roughly torn
10 green beans, cut into small pieces
1 carrot, cut into 1 cm (½ in) cubes
60 g (2 oz) peas, fresh or frozen
1 tomato, roughly chopped
820 ml (28 fl oz) water
½ teaspoon turmeric powder
1 teaspoon salt
Handful cilantro (coriander) leaves, chopped

Method

Heat a deep frying pan on medium to high heat and dry roast the semolina for 5 minutes or until fragrant. Remove from heat and transfer to a plate to cool.

Wipe the pan clean, then heat the ghee or oil in the pan for a minute. Add the mustard seeds and as they start to pop, add cinnamon, bay leaves and cardamom, stir for 30 seconds. Then add the onion, ginger, chillies and curry leaves, stir for a minute. Add all the vegetables and tomato, stir for another minute. Add water, turmeric powder and salt, stir the ingredients well to combine.

When the water starts to boil add the dry roasted semolina, a few spoonfuls at a time, stirring to remove any lumps. Once all the semolina has been added, lower the heat, cover the pan and simmer for 5 minutes until the semolina has absorbed all the water and the vegetables are cooked.

Turn off the heat and gently stir through cilantro leaves.

South Indian Pancakes

Dosai

(Crispy Rice and Lentil Pancake)

Makes: 10–15 pancakes
Cooking Difficulty: Hard

Dosai is South India's answer to the breads of the north or the crepes from Europe. Made from rice and urad dhal, it is soaked, ground and fermented and cooked to produce a thin crispy pancake commonly eaten for breakfast or lunch.

Served with a side of Sambar (page 131) and Coconut Chutney (page 242) is a meal that everyone should try at least once in their life.

Ingredients
310 g (10.6 oz) long grain rice
105 g (3.7 oz) urad dhal, whole
½ teaspoon fenugreek seeds
½ teaspoon salt
6-8 tablespoons canola oil
1 small onion, cut in half

Method
Preparing the batter
Soak the rice, urad dhal and fenugreek seeds in a large bowl covered with 4 cm (1½ in) of cold water for 3 to 4 hours.

Drain the rice and urad dhal reserving the soaking water. Divide into two batches, then place one batch in a powerful blender along with 120 ml (4 fl oz) of the reserved water and process to get a thick coarse batter. Add extra water a few tablespoons at a time if needed. The batter will be a bit grainy, when you rub the batter between your fingers it should feel like fine sand. Repeat for the second batch.

Pour batter into a large bowl, the bowl will need at least 10 cm (4 in) of space above the batter so it has room to ferment and rise. Add salt and an extra 120 ml (4 fl oz) of water, mix well.

Cover with a lid and allow it to rest in a warm place for about 8 to 9 hours, until the batter has risen significantly. Once the batter has risen to the top of the bowl it's ready to be used. You can either use it straight away or put it in the fridge in an airtight container to use later, it will keep for four days in the fridge.

Making the Dosai
Heat a cast iron or heavy based frying pan on medium-high heat. The pan needs to be quite hot, if you sprinkle a little bit of water it should sizzle. Drizzle a teaspoon of oil on the pan and spread on the surface using an onion cut in half or a bit of paper towel.

Using a metal ladle pour a large spoonful of batter, about 120 ml (4 fl oz), on to the centre of the pan and gently make circular motions to spread the batter out and make a large 20 cm (8 in) circle, like a thin crepe. If the batter is too thick it may not spread easily, add a bit to the batter until you get a smoother consistency to work with. Immediately drizzle oil around the edges and around the circles of the dosai, for a richer taste use ghee instead of oil.

When you see the edges of the dosai turning golden brown it's ready to be flipped. Using a metal spatula, gently lift the edges of the circle before lifting the whole dosai. Cook on the other side for another minute. Flip it over once more, then roll into a tube and transfer to a serving plate. Repeat with the rest of the batter, in between each dosai refresh the pan with a bit of oil and rub the pan with a cut onion or paper towel.

You can freeze any excess batter for up to two months.

Masala Dosai
(Crispy Rice Lentil Pancake Filled with Spicy Potatoes)

Makes: 10–15 pancakes
Cooking Difficulty: Hard

A dosai stuffed with delicately spiced bright yellow potatoes, it's one of the most popular ways to eat a dosai. Tastes even better served with Sambar (page 131) and Coconut Chutney (page 242) on the side.

Ingredients
1 portion dosai batter (page 218)
1 portion turmeric and ginger potatoes (page 147)

Method
Heat a cast iron or heavy based frying pan on medium-high heat. The pan needs to be quite hot, if you sprinkle a little bit of water it should sizzle. Using an open cut onion or a bit of paper towel, spread about a tablespoon of oil on the pan.

Using a metal ladle pour a large spoonful of batter, about 120 ml (4 fl oz), on to the centre of the pan and gently make circular motions to spread the batter out and make a large 20 cm (8 in) circle, like a thin crepe. If the batter is too thick it may not spread easily, add a bit of water into the batter until you get a better consistency to work with. Immediately drizzle oil around the edge of the dosai, for a richer taste use ghee instead of oil.

Using a metal spatula gently smooth the batter to create a flat surface. Once the top of the pancake is cooked, take a few scoops of yellow ginger potatoes and spread lengthwise along the middle of the dosai. The bottom of the dosai should be nice and golden brown by now, gently lift up either side of the dosai and fold on top to make a wrap. Transfer to a plate.

Serve hot, with coconut chutney and sambar.

Repeat the same with the rest of the batter, in between each dosai you might need to refresh the pan either with an open cut onion or a bit of paper towel dipped in oil.

Thakkali Dosai

(Tangy Tomato Pancake)

Serves: 6–8
Cooking Difficulty: Medium

This was another way my Mum liked to use tomatoes when they were ripe and in season.
It doesn't require the long fermentation process of a traditional dosai as the tomatoes give
a nice acidic flavor.

Served with Coconut Chutney (page 242) and a simple salad it makes a really nice light
meal for breakfast, lunch or dinner.

Ingredients
155 g (5.3 oz) long grain rice
55 g (2 oz) whole urad dhal
3 dried red chillies
3 ripe tomatoes
4 tablespoons cilantro (coriander), stalks and leaves finely chopped
1 teaspoon cumin seeds
½ teaspoon salt
¼ teaspoon asafoetida
6–8 tablespoons ghee or canola oil

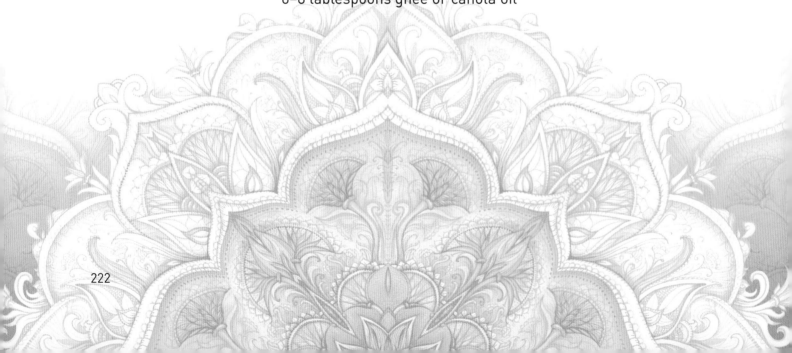

Method

Preparing the batter

Soak rice, urad dhal and dried chilli in a large bowl covered with 4 cm (1½ in) of cold water for 3 to 4 hours. Wash and drain, reserving the soaking water.

Place soaked rice, urad dhal and tomatoes with 120 ml (4 fl oz) of the reserved water in a powerful blender and process to get a coarse batter. Transfer to a large bowl, add cilantro leaves, cumin seeds, salt, and asafoetida, mix well.

Cover the bowl with a plate and place in a warm place for an hour until small bubbles appear. You can prepare the batter ahead of time and store it in the fridge until you're ready to cook the dosai. It will keep in the fridge for a week or longer in the freezer.

Making the thakali dosai

Heat a cast iron or heavy based frying pan on medium-high heat. The pan needs to be quite hot, if you sprinkle a little bit of water it should sizzle. Drizzle a teaspoon of oil on the pan and spread on the surface using an onion cut in half or a bit of paper towel.

Using a metal ladle pour a large spoonful of batter, about 120 ml (4 fl oz), onto the centre of the pan and gently make circular motions to spread the batter out and make a large 20 cm (8 in) circle. Immediately drizzle oil around the edges and around the circles of the thakali dosai, for a richer taste use ghee instead of oil.

After about 2 minutes use a metal spatula to lift up the thakali dosai, check the bottom of the pancake is brown and then flip over to cook the other side for a minute or so until crispy.

Adai

(Chilli, Rice and Lentil Pancake)

Makes: 8–10 pancakes
Cooking Difficulty: Medium

With the addition of channa and toor dhal, Adai is like the healthier cousin of Dosai. It's also easier to make, as it doesn't require fermentation, so my Dad got Mum to make it quite often.

We either had it as a full meal with Morkuzhambu (page 123) or Avial (page 115), or as a snack with honey (trust me it's delicious).

Ingredients
155 g (5.3 oz) long grain rice
70 g (2.4 oz) urad dhal
65 g (2.2 oz) channa dhal or yellow split pea
85 g (3 oz) toor dhal
20 curry leaves
4 tablespoons cilantro (coriander), leaves and stalks chopped
6 dried red chillies
¾ teaspoon salt
¼ teaspoon asafoetida
4 tablespoons ghee or oil (for cooking)

Method
For the batter
Soak rice, urad dhal and channa dhal in a large bowl covered with 4 cm (1½ in) of cold water for 3 hours. Rinse and drain, reserving soaking water.

Place all the rice and dhals, curry leaves, cilantro, dried red chillies, salt and asafoetida in a bowl and mix. In two batches place in a powerful blender with 120 ml (4 fl oz) of reserved water and process to get a thick coarse batter. You can make this ahead of time and store in fridge until you're ready to make the adai. It will keep well in the fridge for a week or longer in the freezer.

continued over the page...

Cooking the adai

Heat a cast iron or heavy based frying pan on medium-high heat. The pan needs to be quite hot, if you sprinkle a little bit of water it should sizzle. Drizzle a teaspoon of oil on the pan and spread on the surface using an onion cut in half or a bit of paper towel.

Using a metal ladle pour a large spoonful of batter, about 120 ml (4 fl oz), onto the centre of the pan and gently make circular motions to spread the batter out and make a large 20 cm (8 in) circle. Immediately drizzle oil around the edges and around the circles of the dosai, for a richer taste use ghee instead of oil.

After about 2 minutes use a metal spatula to lift up the adai, check the bottom of the pancake is brown and then flip over to cook the other side for a minute or so until crispy.

Pesarattu
(Green Mung Bean Pancake)

Makes: 12 to 15 pancakes
Cooking Difficulty: Medium

This was another recipe my Dad picked up on his travels, he liked it because it was made with mung beans and only used a little bit of spice. It's a dish that soon became a regular on our rotation of Indian pancakes. Tomato chutney is perfect with these delicious pancakes.

Pesarattu is a native dish of Andhara Pradesh where they eat it for breakfast with a cup of sweet milky chai (page 268).

Ingredients
175 g (6.1 oz) whole green mung beans
1 teaspoon cumin seeds
2.5 cm (1 in) piece ginger, chopped
4 tablespoons cilantro (coriander), leaves and stalks finely chopped
2 small hot green chillies
½ teaspoon salt
6–8 tablespoons ghee or canola oil

Method
Preparing the batter
Soak the mung beans in a large bowl covered with 4 cm (1½ in) of cold water for 4 to 6 hours, until soft enough that when you press a mung bean between your fingers the skin easily slips off.

Drain the mung beans, reserving about 120 ml (4 fl oz) of the soaking water. Place the soaked mung beans, cumin, ginger, cilantro, chillies and salt in a powerful blender along with 60 ml (2 fl oz) of the reserved water. Process to a coarse batter, it should be like a thick grainy pancake mix, add extra water as needed. If you're using a smaller blender you may need to grind the mix in a few batches. Transfer to a bowl and set aside for 2 hours in a warm place.

continued over the page…

Making the pesarattu

Heat a cast iron or heavy based frying pan on medium heat. The pan needs to be quite hot, if you sprinkle a little bit of water it should sizzle. Drizzle a teaspoon of oil on the pan and spread on the surface using an onion cut in half or a bit of paper towel.

Using a metal ladle pour a large spoonful of batter, about 120 ml (4 fl oz), on to the centre of the pan and gently make circular motions to spread the batter out and make a 20 cm (8 in) circle. If the batter is too thick, it may not easily spread, add a bit of water into the batter until you get a better consistency to work with. Immediately drizzle oil around the edges and around the circles of the pesarattu, for a richer taste you can use ghee instead of oil.

Allow to pesarattu to cook for about 2 minutes until the edges are nice and golden brown. Then use a metal spatula to flip over, gently lift the edges all the way around before lifting the whole thing. Cook on the other side for another minute. Turn it over again so the crispy brown side is at the bottom.

Repeat the same with the rest of the batter.

If you have excess batter you can keep it in the fridge for a few days or in the freezer for longer.

Sides

Papaya Pomegranate Salad

Serves: 4 to 6 as part of a full meal
Cooking Difficulty: Easy

This fresh salad is a nice side to accompany any meal. The flavors are refreshing and nice to balance out the spice of the curries.

Ingredients
1 small green papaya, peeled
1 pomegranate
1 tablespoon lemon juice
4 tablespoons cilantro (coriander), leaves and stalks roughly chopped
Salt to taste

Method
Using a mandolin or grater, shred the papaya into thin long strips. Cut the pomegranate in half and, hold over a bowl and tap thee skin with the handle of a wooden spoon to release the red seeds, discarding any white membrane.

Mix the papaya, pomegranate kernels, lemon juice, cilantro leaves and salt in a large mixing bowl. Gently toss, taste for salt and adjust accordingly.

Carrot Salad

Serves: 4–6 as part of a shared meal
Cooking Difficulty: Easy

Another nice refreshing salad to eat on the side of any meal.

Ingredients
2 medium carrots, coarsely grated
2 tomato, diced
1 red onion, finely sliced
Juice of a lemon
4 tablespoons cilantro (coriander), leaves and stalks finely chopped
1 green chilli (optional)
¼ teaspoon salt

Method
Coarsely grate the carrots using the big circle side on the grater. Dice the tomatoes into small cubes. Finely slice the red onion and separate the slices with your fingers.

Mix everything together with the cilantro in a medium size bowl. Have a taste to see if there's enough salt and lemon juice, adjust to your liking.

Beetroot and Tomato Salad

Serves: 4 as part of a shared meal
Cooking Difficulty: Easy

My daughter did a yoga course in India where she stayed in an ashram, practiced yoga and ate 'saatvic' (no garlic, onion or chilli) food for the month. This was one of the salad recipes that she loved and brought back with her.

We served them at a dinner party as an entrée by spooning a few spoons over pappadums. As a meal it tastes really nice for lunch rolled up in a Chapati (page 178) or on the side of any meal.

Ingredients
4 medium to large beetroots, roots and stalks trimmed
35 g (1.2 oz) unsalted peanuts, dry roasted
2 firm tomatoes, diced
1 teaspoon canola oil
½ teaspoon mustard seeds
20 curry leaves
½ teaspoon urad dhal
Pinch of asafoetida
Juice of half a lemon
½ teaspoon salt

continued over the page...

Method

Place the beetroots, skins on, in a large saucepan of cold water over a high heat. Bring to the boil then reduce to a medium heat to simmer. Cook for 45 minutes, or until done. Drain and then refresh in a bowl of cold water for a few minutes. Remove from the water and remove the skin using your fingers, it should easily peel off.

Cut the beetroot into small 1 cm (½ in) cubes, and place in a salad bowl. Add the toasted peanuts and tomatoes to the bowl.

To finish the salad, heat oil in a small frying pan on a medium-high heat. Add mustard seeds when they pop add curry leaves, urad dhal and asafoetida. Stir continually until urad dhal is slightly brown then tip into the salad bowl. Add lemon juice and salt, stir well and adjust lemon and salt to taste.

Mambazha Pachadi

(Sweet and Spicy Mango Chutney)

Makes: 150 g (5 oz)
Cooking Difficulty: Easy

At weddings and special occasions, we often eat a sweet chutney on the side of the food. I wanted to include this recipe as I've found lots of my friends like sweet chutneys and they've loved this too.

It also works well as a dip for any of the snacks.

Ingredients
1 large green mango, peeled and cut into 2.5 cm (1 in) chunks
1 teaspoon canola oil
¼ teaspoon cumin seeds
4 cm (1½ in) piece ginger, cut into thin strips
¼ teaspoon chilli powder
¼ teaspoon turmeric powder
¼ teaspoon salt
50 g (1.7 oz) jaggery or brown sugar
60 ml (2 fl oz) water

Method:
Heat oil in a small saucepan over a medium heat then add cumin seeds, ginger and mango, stir for a minute. Add chilli, turmeric, salt, jaggery and water. Stir well for 2 minutes or until mixture starts to boil. Lower the heat and simmer for 10 minutes, stirring ocassionally. Cook until mango is soft and the liquid has thickened like a chunky jam. Remove from heat and store in a sterilized jar.

Cucumber Raita

Makes: 500 g (17 oz)
Cooking Difficulty: Easy

Most Indian meals are eaten with a bit of yogurt or raita on the side. Not only does it have a nice cooling effect to balance the spices, it also aids with digestion. The following are a few of our favorite raitas.

Raita is simply delicately spiced with a bit of salt and cumin. You can use already ground cumin powder, or if you have time it does taste nicer when you freshly roast and grind cumin seeds yourself, use ¼ teaspoon cumin seeds for the recipe below.

Ingredients
2 small cucumbers
475 ml (1 pint) thick natural yogurt
¼ teaspoon cumin powder
Salt to taste

Method
Chop the cucumber into small 1 cm (½ in) cubes. Whisk the yogurt, cumin powder and salt until smooth. Add the chopped cucumber, mix well. Refrigerate until you're ready to eat.

Variations

Mixed Raita

Ingredients
1 small cucumber
½ carrot
1 tomato
½ red onion
475 ml (1 pint) thick natural yogurt
¼ teaspoon cumin powder
Salt to taste

Method
Chop the cucumber into small 1 cm (½ in) cubes. Peel and finely grate the carrot. Deseed the tomato and finely cube the tomato. Finely dice the onion. Whisk the yogurt, cumin powder and salt until smooth. Add all the vegetables to the yogurt, mix well. Refrigerate until you're ready to eat.

Mint Raita

Ingredients
475 ml (1 pint) thick natural yogurt
2.5 cm (1 in) piece ginger
1 green chilli
8 tablespoons mint leaves
1 tablespoon lemon juice
Salt to taste

Method
Whisk yogurt until smooth. Place ginger, chilli and mint with 1 tablespoon of yogurt in a small blender and process into a paste. Add mint paste and lemon juice to the yogurt, mix well. Taste for salt and adjust to your liking.

Thenga Chutney
(Coconut Chutney)

Makes: 100 ml (3 fl oz)
Cooking Difficulty: Easy

This is a Tamil coconut chutney which you'll always find served with Dosai (page 218). You can also eat it with many snacks like Masala Vada (page 41) or Bonda (page 30).

Ingredients
120 g (4.2 oz) desiccated or fresh grated coconut (page 280)
2.5 cm (1 in) piece ginger, finely grated
1 green chilli
¼ teaspoon salt
120 ml (4 fl oz) warm water
½ teaspoon canola oil
¼ teaspoon black mustard seeds
6 curry leaves, roughly torn

Method
Soak coconut, ginger, green chilli and salt in warm water for 5 minutes. Then place everything in a spice blender and process until you get a coarse paste, transfer to a serving bowl.

Heat the oil in small saucepan, add the mustard seeds, once they start popping turn off the heat, add curry leaves stir for a few seconds, pour over chutney.

Simple Tomato Chutney

Makes: 100 ml (3 fl oz)
Cooking Difficulty: Easy

A simple spicy dip to eat alongside your favorite snacks or South indian pancake, you could even use it as a spread on a sandwich.

Ingredients
3 tablespoons canola oil
1 red onion, thinly sliced
2 cloves garlic
20 curry leaves
½ teaspoon chilli powder
½ teaspoon salt
4 tomatoes, roughly chopped
60 ml (2 fl oz) water

Method
Heat the oil in frying pan over a medium heat. Add the onion and garlic and cook until onion is soft and translucent. Then add the curry leaves, chilli powder, salt and stir well.

Add the tomatoes and water, cook until the tomatoes are soft and release their juices. Turn down the heat and cook for a further 5 to 10 minutes until it turns into a lovely spicy gravy, if it looks more like a paste add more water to make a gravy.

Remove from the heat, transfer to a mixing bowl and allow to cool. Leave it chunky or if you prefer use a hand held blender to make a smoother paste.

Raji's Special Chilli Pickle

Makes: A small jar of pickle
Cooking Difficulty: Hard

This is a recipe only for those brave chilli lovers.

I've always absolutely loved eating chilli in all forms ever since I was a little girl. My grandma used to make a green chilli pickle, that makes my mouth (and eyes!) water just thinking of it.

This chilli pickle is inspired by grandma but I've used red chillies instead of green. Naturally the hotter the chilli you use the hotter this pickle will be.

Ingredients
1 tablespoon dried tamarind
200 g (7 oz) fresh hot red chillies, tops chopped off
3 cloves garlic
2 teaspoons salt
60 ml (2 fl oz) Indian sesame oil (known as gingelly oil available in Indian stores)
1 teaspoon black mustard seeds
25 curry leaves, roughly torn
1 teaspoon asafoetida

continued over the page...

Method

Soak the dried tamarind in 3 tablespoons of warm to hot water for 10 minutes. Squeeze the softened tamarind with your hand and mix the fibres well in the water, strain through a fine sieve pushing as much pulp as you can through, set aside.

Place chillies, tamarind pulp, garlic, salt and a tablespoon of water in a blender and process to a coarse paste.

Heat the Indian sesame oil in a medium size frying pan. Add the mustard seeds and when they pop add the curry leaves, asafoetida and chilli paste, stir for a minute. Take care when you add the curry leaves and chilli paste as they will splutter, and because it's hot chilli you don't want any juice to splash on to you or into your eyes. To be safe wear an apron and stand back a bit from the stove when adding and stirring the chilli.

After a minute, lower the heat as low as possible and slowly simmer for 15 minutes. Cover with a lid, leaving it slightly ajar to release the steam. Stir occasionally to ensure the chilli paste doesn't stick to the bottom of the pan. When the oil starts to separate from the paste, it's ready. Turn the heat off and cool. Store in a sterilized jar, it will keep for up to 3 weeks.

Red Garlic Chilli Chutney

Cooking Difficulty: Easy

This sweet chilli chutney tastes perfect when spread on Masala Dosai (page 220) or Vada Pav (page 68), you could also use it as a dip with your favorite snack or even as a spread to make a spicy sandwich.

Ingredients
1 teaspoon canola oil
6 cloves garlic, sliced
2 teaspoons chilli powder
50 g (1.7 oz) desiccated or fresh grated coconut (page 280)
¼ teaspoon salt
3 tablespoons water

Method
Heat the oil in a small frying pan on medium-high heat. Add the garlic and cook until golden. Remove from the heat and cool. Place garlic, chilli powder, coconut and salt and 3 tablespoons of water in a spice grinder and process to a smooth paste.

Store in a sterilized jar, it will keep for 5 days.

Sweets

Carrot Halwa

(Carrot Pudding)

Serves: 4–6
Cooking Difficulty: Medium

There are many kinds of halwas that appear all across India, they're either based on semolina (Rava Kesari page 265) or like this with a vegetable like carrot. Cooked with ghee and sugar, you get a sweet and moist pudding best served warm with a little ice cream.

Ingredients
8 tablespoons ghee
400 g (14 oz) grated carrot
120 ml (4 fl oz) milk
225 g (8 oz) white sugar
50 g (1.7 oz) ground almond
50 g (1.7 oz) almond flakes, crushed into small pieces
5 green cardamom pods, skins discarded seeds ground into a powder
1 teaspoon pistachios, thinly sliced

Method
Heat 3 tablespoons of ghee in a non-stick pan on medium-high heat, add the grated carrot and cook for 2 minutes, stirring constantly. Add the milk and sugar and continue to cook for another 2 minutes, stir occasionally. When the milk starts to boil, add the ground almond, half the almond flakes and ground cardamom powder, mix well.

Lower the heat and cook the carrot mixture for 20 minutes until the milk has fully evaporated and the carrots are completely cooked. Stir frequently to ensure the carrot doesn't burn.

Finally add the rest of the ghee and cook for 2 more minutes, it should be a rich orange moist pudding by now. You can mash it up further to get a completely smooth consistency or leave it as is if you prefer a bit of texture.

Remove from the heat and transfer to a serving dish and garnish with the remaining almond flakes.

Gulab Jamun
(Golden Milk Dumplings in Rosewater Syrup)

Makes: 25
Cooking Difficulty: Medium

Gulab jamun's are probably the most famous Indian sweet, but I'm never really happy with the ones I've eaten out. Made fresh these are just a beautiful dessert to serve and are an absolute favorite of all my friends and family, you have to take care when deep frying the balls to cook at a good even temperature, to prevent burning.

Serve with ice cream and strawberries for afternoon tea or to end a meal.

Ingredients
Rose water syrup
335 g (11.8 oz) sugar
240 ml (8 fl oz) water
Few strands saffron
2 whole green cardamom pods
1 teaspoon rose water

Golden milk dumplings
125 g (4.4 oz) milk powder
35 g (1.2 oz) self-raising flour
¼ teaspoon cardamom powder
1 tablespoon almond flakes, coarsely ground
80 ml (3 fl oz) full fat cream
1 tablespoon pistachios, coarsely ground
Canola oil for deep frying

continued over the page...

Method

Syrup

First make the syrup. Boil the sugar, water, saffron and cardamom together on medium-high heat for 10 minutes or until you get a thick syrup. Remove from the heat, add rose water and set aside. Pour the syrup to a shallow dish large enough to hold all the gulab jamuns.

Dumpling dough

Place the milk powder, flour, cardamom and almond flakes in a large mixing bowl and mix together using a whisk to get rid of any lumps. Now add the cream and mix to create a crumbly dough. Divide into 20 portions, then using your hands roll each one into a smooth round ball and place on to a plate. If there are any cracks in the balls use a bit of milk to moisten your hands, which will help to smooth out the balls. Cover the rolled balls with plastic wrap or a tea towel to prevent them from drying out.

Frying the dumplings

Fill a deep frying pan two thirds full with canola oil, heat on a medium heat. When cooking gulab jamuns the temperature of the oil is crucial. To test if the oil is the right temperature, take a small pinch of dough and drop it in the oil, if the oil is the right temperature it should sink to the bottom of the pan and then after a few seconds slowly rise to the top. If the crumb immediately starts to sizzle the oil is too hot, remove from the heat for few minutes to bring the temperature down, then put it back on the heat and test the temperature again.

Cook 5 to 6 gulab jamuns at a time. When fried they double up in size so give plenty of space for each dumpling. Cook for about 2 minutes, frequently turning so they cook evenly and are a lovely deep golden brown all over. Once they're the right color, lift from oil and drain on paper towel for a minute.

Gently drop the dumplings into the warm syrup making sure they are well covered in the syrup. You should let the gulab jamuns soak for 1 to 2 hours so they get nice and moist and soak up all the lovely syrup.

You can store the gulab jamuns in the fridge for up to a week and serve chilled or warm with a sprinkling of pistashios.

Kheer

(Rice Pudding with Almonds and Pistachios)

Serves: 4–6
Cooking Difficulty: Easy

Kheer is a warming and sweet rice pudding, like most Indian dishes there are lots of different versions but I've opted to share a Northern Indian version as it's rich but not as sweet as its southern counterparts. The added nuts give a bit of texture and balance to the dish.

Ingredients
30 g (1 oz) almonds
30 g (1 oz) pistachios, plus 2 tablespoons for garnish
50 g (1.7 oz) rice
1 litre (2 pints) milk
110 g (3.8 oz) sugar
6 whole green cardamom, skins discarded and seeds ground into a powder
¼ teaspoon saffron threads

Method
Soak the almonds and pistachios in warm water for 1 hour. Push the almonds out of their skins, roughly chop both the almonds and pistachios set aside.

Soak the rice for 10 minutes, wash and drain. Place drained rice on a board, cover with a kitchen towel and gently crush using a rolling pin, to break the rice up a bit.

Heat the milk in a large saucepan over a medium heat. As the milk starts to boil add the crushed rice, sugar and chopped nuts, stir well to ensure rice isn't stuck to the bottom of the pan. Lower the heat and cook for 30 minutes stirring occasionally. If the rice and milk boils over reduce the heat.

The kheer is cooked when the milk has reduced by half and the rice is soft. Remove from heat and finally stir through saffron and cardamom.

Transfer to a serving dish. Garnish with the remaining pistachios.

Pasi Paruppu Payassum
(Yellow Mung Dhal Pudding)

Serves: 4–6
Cooking Difficulty: Easy

For special occasions we usually eat a full meal, several vegetable dishes, a few courses of curries and rice, all eaten on a banana leaf. But the first thing to hit the leaf is a small spoon of sweet payassum. If you want more you get given it in a little cup to eat throughout or at the end of the meal.

If you can, buy some jaggery from your local Indian store as it adds a different kind of flavor than brown sugar, and believe it or not, unlike it's refined sugar counterparts actually has quite a few health benefits.

Ingredients
110 g (3.8 oz) yellow moong dhal
240 ml (8 fl oz) water
6 whole green cardamom, skins discarded seeds ground into a powder
100 g (3.5 oz) jaggery or brown sugar
240 ml (8 fl oz) coconut milk
2 tablespoons ghee
1 tablespoon cashews, broken into small pieces
25 g (0.8 oz) dried coconut flakes

Method
Dry roast the moong dhal in a small frying pan on a low-medium heat until golden brown, stirring to ensure it doesn't burn. Transfer to a plate and let it cool.

Wash roasted dhal and drain. Place dhal in a small saucepan with 240 ml (8 fl oz) of water, cook on medium-high heat until mung dhal is very soft. Lower the heat and mash the dhal into a paste using a potato masher. Then add cardamom powder, jaggery or brown sugar and mix well. Cook for 5 minutes, you should get a thick brown liquid. Add coconut milk, stir well and cook on low heat for 10 minutes. Remove from the heat.

Heat ghee in a small frying pan on medium heat. Add cashews and dried coconut, cook until it turns golden brown, pour over the payasam.

Mysorepak
(Crumbly Besan Flour Fudge)

Makes: 20 pieces
Cooking Difficulty: Hard

This South Indian sweet is almost like a shortbread crossed with fudge, it's sweet and buttery and melts in your mouth. A little square with a cup of tea is just perfect.

There's only a few ingredients, but it's all about technique with this recipe, using hot ghee creates a smooth texture, and getting the syrup to be quite stringy results in a more bubbly final product.

Ingredients
65 g (2.3 oz) besan flour
220 g (7.7 oz) ghee
225 g (7.9 oz) sugar
60 ml (4 fl oz) water

Method
Prepare a square or rectangle casserole dish or baking tray 18 x 20 cm (7 x 8 in) or 20 x 20 cm (8 x 8 in) and grease with a bit of ghee.

Heat frying pan on a medium heat and toast the besan flour for 2 minutes stirring constantly. Pass the toasted flour through a fine sieve, cool.

Melt the ghee in a small saucepan, until hot but not boiling.

Place sugar and water in a deep frying pan over a medium-high heat, stir continuously. Bring to a slow boil and allow the sugar syrup to bubble for 2 minutes. Reduce the heat to low, and use a whisk to gradually stir in the besan flour until you get a smooth paste.

Put the saucepan with the ghee back on an extremely low heat to keep it warm.

continued over the page...

Now add one tablespoon of ghee at a time, stirring with a wooden spoon for 2 minutes to fully incorporate the ghee and thicken the mixture, before adding the next spoon. Once you've used most of the ghee the mixture will start to change texture and become frothy, at that point take the pan off the heat and pour into the prepared tray.

Pat the mixture down with a flat spatula so it's completely even, then allow to set which should take about 10 minutes.

Once it's cooled and hardened you can cut the mysorepak into squares. Store in an airtight container, it will keep for a few weeks.

Shrikhand

(Thick Yogurt with Cardamom, Saffron and Pistachio)

Makes: 500 g (17 oz)
Cooking Difficulty: Easy

I first tried shrikhand at a Marathi friend's house who had included it as part of her Diwali feast. The yogurt gets hung and mixed in with sugar and saffron making a delightfully thick and creamy dessert. It's really easy to make, you just need to prepare it ahead of time to give the yogurt plenty of time to drain.

It's become one of my favorite desserts to make and loved by many of my friends, when I make it in summer I make a mango puree and fold it through, because who doesn't love mango?

Ingredients
1 kg (2.2 lb) greek yogurt
190 g (6.5 oz) caster sugar
4 tablespoon pistachios, finely sliced
5 cardamom pods, skins discarded and seeds ground to a powder
¼ teaspoon saffron threads

To make this you'll also need muslin or cheesecloth, a strainer and a large mixing bowl.

continued over the page...

Method

Place a strainer in a large mixing bowl, ensuring there's a gap of at least 10 cm (4 in) to allow the whey to drip. Then lay the muslin cloth out over the strainer, allowing extra fabric to fall of the edge.

Spoon yogurt on to the cloth, bring the edges of the cloth together and tie tightly with kitchen twine to make a tight parcel. Drain overnight and up to 24 hours until all the whey is drained and you're left with a thick ball of yogurt.

Transfer yogurt to a large mixing bowl, add the sugar, 3 tablespoons of the pistachios, cardamom and saffron. Give it a good whisk until you have a thick creamy yogurt.

Pour into a bowl or individual ramekins and garnish with remaining 1 tablespoon pistachios.

If you're adding mango, make a thick mango puree by blending 2 ripe mangoes, and either fold that through the shrikhand or put a dollop on top of individual bowls.

Rava Kesari

(Semolina Pudding with Saffron and Cashews)

Serves: 6–8
Cooking Difficulty: Easy

This South Indian sweet is a kind of halwa based on semolina flour. It's usually colored bright orange from food coloring, but my Dad didn't like using synthetic ingredients so he got Mum to use a bit of saffron instead, giving it a light yellow color and fragrance.

It has a spongy texture that melts in your mouth, you also get texture from the nuts. A popular version of this dish includes pineapple, it's a simple variation as you add 40 g (1.5 oz) of roughly chopped pineapple when you add the semolina.

Ingredients
225 g (7.9 oz) sugar
6 green cardamom pods, seeds ground into a powder and skins kept
8–10 saffron threads
110 g (3.8 oz) ghee
165 g (5.8 oz) semolina
35 g (1.2 oz) whole cashews, finely chopped
1 tablespoon dried sultanas (optional)

Method
Heat the sugar with 475 ml (1 pint) of water, cardamom powder and skins and saffron in a small saucepan on medium-high heat. Boil for 5 minutes until the sugar has fully dissolved and it's a lovely yellow color.

Heat half the ghee in a deep frying pan on medium-high heat. Add semolina and cashews and stir for 2 minutes or until semolina turns a very pale golden brown. Then add the sugar syrup, stir well to ensure there are no lumps. If you're adding sultanas add them now. Turn the heat down, cover the pan and cook for 5 minutes until semolina absorbs all the liquid, but is still moist. Add remaining ghee, cook it for another 2 minutes until everything has absorbed.

Spread out onto a greased tray, 4 cm (1½ in) high. Refrigerate, then cut into squares.

Drinks

Sweet Milky Chai

Makes: 2 litres (4 pints)

There are so many different versions of chai but this is the one I've been making at home for years.

Ingredients
1.4 litres (3 pints) water
475 ml (2 pints) milk
4 tablespoons strong tea leaves (Darjeeling or English breakfast works well)
10 green cardamom, whole cloves lightly pounded
4 cloves
2 x 5 cm (2 in) piece cinnamon, broken into half
5 cm (2 in) piece ginger, grated
Sugar or honey, to taste

Method
Place all ingredients in a saucepan on medium-high heat. Bring to the boil and then lower the heat and simmer for 15 minutes. Strain through a fine sieve in a pot, serve with sugar or honey to taste.

Lemon Ginger Cordial

Makes: 500 ml (17 fl oz) of syrup

Lime or lemon soda is popular all over India, this is my twist with a bit of ginger to make a really refreshing summer drink.

Ingredients
570 g (20 oz) sugar
2 x 5 cm (2 in) piece ginger, cut into thin strips
700 ml (1 ½ pints) water
240 ml (8 fl oz) freshly squeezed lemon juice

Method
Place the sugar, ginger and water in a small saucepan and gently boil for 15 minutes to make a thick syrup. Remove from the heat, and stir through the lemon juice. Mix well then pass through a sieve to remove ginger and any pips. Store in a sterilized jar and refrigerate until ready to use. It will keep in the fridge for 2 to 3 weeks.

You can either make a drink with still water or soda. Fill a tall glass half full with ice cubes, add 1 to 2 tablespoons of syrup and top with sparkling or still water.

Strawberry Falooda

Makes: 4–6 glasses

Falooda is a popular summer drink available on most street corners of India, and with all of the elements it could almost be a dessert.

It looks quite fun and magical when it's served, having different layers of black chia seeds, vermicelli noodles and pink rose syrup. Mixed all together the flavors and textures are really refreshing. You can also add a dollop of vanilla ice cream to make it a bit of an afternoon treat.

Ingredients
200 g (7 oz) chopped strawberries
6 tablespoons white sugar
2 tablespoons vermicelli
700 ml (1 ½ pints) milk
2 tablespoons ground almond
2 tablespoons chia seeds (soaked for 30 minutes)

Method
Place the strawberries with 2 tablespoons of sugar in a small saucepan and place on a low-medium heat. Cook for 5 minutes, stirring until strawberries are stewed but haven't completely broken down. Remove from the heat and transfer to a dish.

Heat a non-stick deep frying pan and dry roast vermicelli for 2 minutes until it starts to change color. Add the milk and sugar, bring to a boil turn then lower the heat and simmer for 10 minutes until vermicelli is cooked. Add the ground almonds and simmer for another minute. Remove from the heat and let it cool.

Refrigerate everything, the soaked chia seeds, milk and strawberries until completely cool.

Serve in small glasses, layering 2 tablespoons of the stewed strawberries, then 2 teaspoons of chia seeds and 120 ml (4 fl oz) of the sweet vermicelli milk. If you like, top it up with a scoop of ice cream and coconut flakes.

Mango Lassi

Makes: 4–6 glasses

Make this refreshing drink when you can get your hands on really ripe and sweet mangoes
it makes all the difference.

Ingredients
475 ml (16 fl oz) thick greek yogurt
240 ml (8 fl oz) buttermilk
300 g (10.5 oz) ripe sweet mango, chopped and chilled
6 ice cubes
4 tablespoons white sugar

Method
Simply place all ingredients in a blender and process until smooth. Chill and serve.

How To's

Ghee
(Clarified Butter)

Makes: 120 ml (4 fl oz)

Making ghee is surprisingly easy, but does require your full attention so you can pick up on the visual queues and changing sounds, stirring when needed. Once you've melted ghee pour it into a sterilized jar, it will last for a few weeks to a month.

Ingredients
250 g (9 oz) good quality unsalted butter

Method
Place butter in a small heavy based saucepan on medium-high heat. Stir to encourage the butter to melt.

Once the butter has melted reduce the heat slightly to a medium heat. Stir, and then wait for a thick white foam to form. That foam will start to bubble away and you'll slowly see the milk proteins starting to separate, stir a few times to encourage even cooking.

After a minute or two, that thick froth will dissipate and the butter will start to bubble and look clearer, stir every 20 seconds or so. The bubbles will start forming and popping quicker and quicker, going from small bubbles to bigger ones, keep stirring to encourage this process and to prevent burning.

After the bubbles have gotten quite big, the next moment they'll disappear and turn into a light and airy froth that quickly rises. Immediately turn the heat off, this is a sign the ghee is done. Keep stirring to prevent the froth from boiling over.

Allow to settle and cool for a few minutes before straining through a fine sieve lined with muslin into a sterilized jar. Straining through muslin will remove any of those solids that got more cooked, but if you don't have a sieve these golden brown solids will just settle to the bottom of the jar and do no harm to the rest of the ghee.

Paneer

(Indian Cottage Cheese)

Makes: 400–500 g (14–17 oz) of Paneer

Paneer is the only cheese used in Indian cooking. Making it from scratch is surprisingly easy. Give it a go, I promise you won't regret it!

Ingredients
2 litres (4 pints) full cream milk, good quality fresh milk*
3 tablespoons fresh lemon juice, plus extra 2 tablespoons if needed

*It is important to use fresh milk as UHT milk won't separate. You can use a low fat milk but the paneer won't be as rich and creamy.

Method
Gently heat milk in a large saucepan over a medium-high heat. Stir frequently so the milk doesn't form a skin or scald.

As soon the milk starts to boil and rise, remove from the heat and add the lemon juice. The milk should curdle immediately, add more lemon juice if it doesn't completely curdle. The curds will separate from the whey. Let the milk stand for 10 to 15 minutes, until the curds have completely separated from the liquid, it will look quite watery.

Set up a strainer over a large bowl and line with muslin or cheesecloth. Pour the mixture into the strainer. Allow most of the whey to drain away into the bowl (you can use this whey in any other baking recipe), then bring the edges of the muslin together, twist and squeeze.

Place the tightly squeezed package on a plate, press down a bit and shape roughly into a square. Then press down with another plate with a 1kg weight on top, you could use a mortar or a large jar filled with rice. Press for 1 hour.

Unwrap the cloth, and the paneer is ready to use straight away for your chosen dish. You can also store the paneer in fresh water in an airtight container for up to two days.

Yogurt

Makes: 1 litre (2 pints)

Traditionally Indian families always made their yogurt at home with the left over milk from the day. It's a bit more sour than normal yogurt but like anything made from scratch tastes wonderfully light and fresh.

Ingredients
1 litre (2 pints) milk
2 tablespoons Greek yogurt (used as culture)

Method
Gently heat milk in a 1.5 litre (3 pints) saucepan on medium-high heat. As soon as the milk starts to boil, lower the heat to simmer for 2 minutes. Remove from heat and pour into a large bowl. Allow the milk to cool down until just warm to the touch, then add the yogurt culture and stir well. Cover with a plate, wrap it in a towel for insulation and keep it in a warm place like the oven (not turned on), overnight.

By the morning the yogurt should have set, you can taste a little bit, home made yogurt is usually a bit more watery and sour than store bought yogurt. If it still tastes a bit milky leave it out for a bit longer.

Refrigerate and eat in the next 3 to 4 days. You can then use a little bit of this yogurt as culture for your next batch.

Making the Perfect Rice

Making fluffy rice can, for some, feels more complicated than it actually is. Here's a simple way that we prepare rice, which will guarantee fluffy results every time. The quality of rice really does make the difference, because we eat so much rice in our diet we tend to go to the Indian store and buy a 5 kg (11 lb) bag of a high grade basmati rice. Supermarkets are more regularly stocking a larger range, try to get the best quality one you can get your hands on.

Ingredients
400 g (14 oz) good quality basmati rice
1 litre (2 pints) water

Method
Wash the rice thoroughly until the water runs clear. This removes the starch from the rice, preventing it from being gluggy and sticky.

Cover the rice with plenty of cold water and soak for 15 to 20 minutes, drain. Soaking the rice makes each grain of rice really long when cooked.

Drain the rice then place it in a 2 litre (4 pint) saucepan. Add water, stir well making sure the surface of the rice is even.

Place on a medium-high heat and bring to the boil. Lower the heat, cover with a lid and simmer for 15 minutes. You'll know the rice is cooked when the grains of rice start to stand upright. Never stir rice while it's cooking. Once cooked gently tip it out onto a platter and use a fork to fluff up the rice, allow to steam.

Grating Fresh Coconut

We use a lot of coconut in our food in Tamil cuisine. Whether it's to lightly season vegetables or create spice blends used in different curries. Grating your own coconut does take a bit of effort but it's well worth it for the taste. You can also buy special coconut grating tools which actually make the process relatively straightforward.

If you can't get your hands on a fresh coconut you can use desiccated coconut, just soak it in a bit of warm water to soften it up a bit and use as called for in the recipe. Indian shops also often sell fresh grated coconut in their freezer section.

More and more supermarkets and good green grocers are stocking coconuts. A good coconut will be a bit heavy, shake it close to your ear and listen for the water inside, if you see any signs of moulds on the eye don't buy the coconut.

Method

Run the coconut under cold water, pulling off most of the strands of the coconut hanging on the outside. Then locate the eyes of the coconut, the three depressions on one of the sides, hold the coconut in your hand by placing your middle fingers on those eyes and your thumb on the other end.

Hold the coconut over a bowl, then use the dull side of a cleaver and hit the coconut across the middle several times turning the coconut as you go until it cracks all the way around. All the coconut juice will drip into the bowl, which makes a refreshing drink.

If you have a coconut grater use that to grate the flesh of the coconut. If not there are a few extra steps you need to follow below.

Place the coconut in a 200°C (400°F) oven for 20 minutes, this helps separate the flesh from the shell. When the coconut halves have cooled down use the point of a knife to pry the flesh out of the shelf.

Use a peeler to remove the skin on the coconut meat, so you're just left with the white meat.

Then cut into manageable pieces, and then grate on the small hole side of the grater.

Place in a zip lock bag and use that day for any recipe, or freeze and use as needed.

Spice Powders

Garam Masala

Makes: 50 g (2 oz)

Garam masala is probably the most known Indian spice blend, there are lots of ways to make it and this blend is the one that I have been making for years. Once you've made it you can store it in the freezer, which will keep it at its freshest. If you are going to buy a pre-made garam masala, I'd encourage you to get it from somewhere making it in small fresh batches like a whole food stores, but do have a go at making it yourself as it is so easy.

Ingredients
4 tablespoons cilantro (coriander) seeds
24 whole green cardamom pods
20 whole cloves
4 x 4 cm (1.5 in) cinnamon sticks

Method
Place all the ingredients, keeping the cardamom skins on, in a spice grinder and process to a fine powder. Store in a sterilized airtight jar in a cool and dark place, it will keep fresh for 2 months.

Sambar Powder

Makes: 110 g (4 oz)

Sambar powder is a spice commonly used in the south to flavor curries and vegetables. In India my sister-in-law freshly roasts all the ingredients at home and then sends it off to the mill where the local shop will grind it all into a coarse but fine powder. For those of us who don't have a local mill, a simple spice or coffee grinder will do.

Ingredients
30 g (1 oz) cilantro (coriander) seeds
1 tablespoon channa dhal or yellow split peas
1 tablespoon toor dhal
1 teaspoon yellow moong dhal
1 teaspoon turmeric powder
6 tablespoons hot chilli powder (adjust to taste)

Method
Place all the cilantro seeds, channa dhal, toor dhal and yellow moong dhal in a small heavy based frying pan on a medium heat. Stir frequently and dry roast for 3 minutes, transfer to a plate and cool.

Place the roasted spices along with the turmeric and chilli powder into a spice grinder and process to a fine powder. Cool before storing in a sterilized airtight jar in a cool and dark place, it will keep fresh for 2 months.

Index

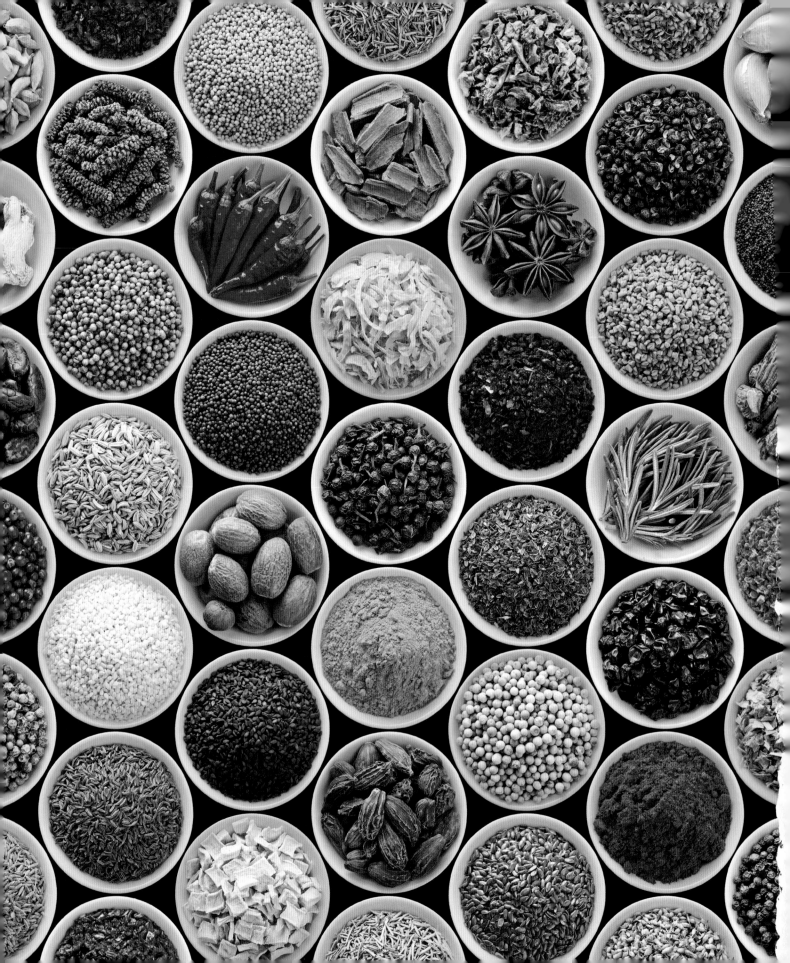